(handwritten inscription): To Barbara, A Truly remarkable and loving woman of God To God Be The Glory. Love, Nevalon Mitchell Feb. 18, 2006

The Liberation of
The Black Church and
The Preacher

*Overcoming Tradition through
Kingdom Principles*

Dr. Nevalon Mitchell, Jr.

The Liberation of The Black Church and The Preacher

Overcoming Tradition through Kingdom Principles

Dr. Nevalon Mitchell, Jr.

PUBLISHED BY:
BRENTWOOD CHRISTIAN PRESS
4000 BEALLWOOD AVENUE
COLUMBUS, GEORGIA 31904

*This book is dedicated to the memory
of my son,
Nevalon Mitchell III, "Toot"
and to my parents
Deacon Nevalon and Emma Rena Mitchell, Sr.
They gave me to the Lord before I was born
and
gave the Lord to me after I was born.*

Acknowledgements

I am eternally indebted to many persons for assistance, encouragement and support in the completion of this project. Dr. Lewis V. Baldwin, a trusted and devoted friend and brother, and Dr. John M. Alexander, Jr., Preacher – Pastor par excellence, were extremely helpful in words and deeds. I cannot begin to say enough about the importance of Dr. Lewis V. Baldwin's expertise and direction in my research and writing. He often interrupted his busy teaching schedule at Vanderbilt University to telephone me and send valuable information that supported the completion of this work. He and his wife Jackie (my sister) allowed me to share their home on two different occasions when I went to Nashville to research and write. To both of them I extend my love, appreciation and gratitude. To my word processors, Mary Bates-Washington and Betsy Cagle I give my thanks for a great job. To my very dear friend Reverend Dr. H. L. Jones – thanks for everything.

These acknowledgements would be incomplete without some reference to the constant prayers, love and support of my "sweet song at midnight"; Kaye, my devoted and lovely wife. Most of all I want to thank almighty God for giving me the intelligence; the will and the determination to finish this task and realize this dream.

Contents

About the Book

This book is an attempt to analyze the historic roles of the black church and the black preacher in light of liberation theology of radical social involvement. The first chapter, "The Black Church and the Black Preacher: African Roots, underscores the various ways in which African religious traditions shaped and informed the style and ethos of the black church, and the authority and artistic creativity of the black preacher. Only fleeting attention has been given the black preacher in this regard. Some attention is devoted in this chapter to how the image of Africa, as reflected in the early black church and the black preacher, contributed to a liberation theology that would find a strong intellectual character centuries later.

Chapter two covers the different images of the black church and the black preacher during slavery. It is called, "Spiritual and Artistic Forms: The Black Church and the Black Preacher During Slavery." Emphasis is placed on how the black church translated its liberation theology into practical reality through its roles as the "Old Israel" and the "All-Comprehending Institution." The Church's involvement in Abolitionists activity, the Underground Railroad, and other movements against slavery and racism is regarded as an early expression of liberation theology. The preacher's significance as a symbol of hope, a leader in the spiritual destiny of the folk, an agent of protest, and a fashioner and exemplar of culture is also interpreted within this context.

Chapter three begins with the immediate postbellum period and extends to the present, with a special focus on the implications of black church activism and black preaching for contemporary liberation theology. The argument is that the church and preachers in the slave songs, sermons, tales, and other

6

sources. This chapter is entitled, "Beyond Slavery: The Black Church and the Black Preacher Since Slavery."

The next chapter discusses black women in the ministry of the black church. It treats this as the most significant challenge confronting the black church with its strong tradition of a male-dominated leadership. The growing assertiveness of black women in the black church, and the extent to which gender issues are currently shaping black theology, is the central thrust of this chapter. It is called, "Extending the Tradition: Black Women and Ministry in the Black Church." This fourth chapter underscores the need for African-Americans to rethink the traditions of the black church and the black preacher in light of issues that are currently being raised in the works of Delores Williams, Jacquelyn Grant, Marcia Riggs, and other womanist theologians.

The fifth chapter is entitled, "Blazing New Paths: Challenges Confronting the Black Church and Its Leadership in the Future." Here the stress is on the need for new and more vital ministries and missions to address drug addiction, Aids, poverty, illiteracy, and other problems that are still negatively affecting the quality of life in the African-American community.

Foreword

I thank God for the wisdom and talent he has given to Lieutenant Colonel Nevalon Mitchell, Jr., as evidenced by this book on the traditions of the church and the preacher. After thirty-seven years of pastoral endeavors, I can say from experience that this book serves as an outstanding chronicle of the historical role of the black church and the black preacher. Knowledge of the rich heritage of the black church and the black pastor both enrichens and shapes our understanding of present day experience. It also builds a reservoir of information to serve as a fortifying foundation for future generations.

Chaplain Mitchell begins his work with references to African religious tradition and its role in shaping black church and the experience of the black preacher. He traces this legacy of the black church and the black preacher during slavery by documenting their roles as symbols of hope through the most harrowing experience of history. The author's trek takes the reader beyond slavery and to the present still building on the rich theological traditions of the past. Rather than ignore the discussion, Chaplain Mitchell tackles the role of black women in the ministry of the black church and proposes extending the tradition to include rather than exclude women in the ministry as a liberating forces in the black church. No longer, he expresses, can afford to apply narrow interpretations of the Bible in an attempt to limit the abilities and potential of women; if we do we are no better than those whose methods of oppression have shaped much of our experience.

In looking forward, Chaplain Mitchell emphasizes the need for stronger ministries and missions to address many of the challenges humankind will face in the future; those challenges that will affect the quality of life in the African-American community.

This book provides a comprehensive reflection, analysis and projection of the major issues that have faced and will face the black church and the black preacher as we close the twenty-first century and enter the new millennium. In recounting major historical experiences, the author allow the reader to identify with the total black experience as it relates to the church and its leadership--past, present and future.

I believe this inspired book can truly serve as a catalyst for change in the black church and in our communities if readers allow the information to jolt their thinking and envelop their beliefs about the black church and the black preacher.

John M Alexander, Jr.
St. John United Baptist Church
Northwest Washington, District of Columbia

Introduction

My critical analysis of black liberation theology as an intellectual discipline has been shaped and informed by more than twenty years of service as a preacher, pastor, and chaplain in the United States Army. To my knowledge, no African American with this background and breadth of experience has offered an extensive critical assessment of black theology and its sources.

Unfortunately, most African American preachers and pastors remain uninformed about developing trends in black theology since the late 1960s, and most black chaplains in the various branches of military service remain too wedded to the status quo to seriously consider this phenomenon as a part of what they do in terms of preaching and teaching.[1]

This book challenges black liberation theology at the point of its sources. It contends that from the origins of black theology with black male thinkers in the 1960s to its maturation with womanist thinkers in the 1980s and 1990s, the traditions of the black church and the black preacher have been assigned less importance as intellectual sources than the writings of major white Western theologians. This "identity crisis" in black theology, as Cecil W. Cone calls it, was evident with the appearance in 1969 of James H. Cone's *Black Theology and Black Power*, the first book-length manuscript on the subject.[2] Black theologians' persistent reliance on white Western theological trends for their insights, categories, and models reflects their need to find acceptance and legitimation in the academy. At the same time, this tendency is such that black theologians must make white Western theological traditions secondary in importance to African American Christian sources. This is the main argument set forth in the pages that follow.

This book consists of five chapters which combine insights from the disciplines of history and theology. In other words, its theoretical framework is rooted in both the history of the black church and its preaching traditions and the kind of existential, folk theology that emerged out of these traditions prior to the rise of black theology in the academy. Chapter one explores the African roots of the black church1md the black preacher, and the relevance and implications of this background for doing black theology. This chapter shows that contemporary black theologians have not taken seriously the debate over African survivals in African American Christianity, one popularized by the black sociologist E. Franklin Frazier and the Jewish cultural anthropologist Melville 1. Herskovits. My contention is that through a serious engagement of the "African survivals question," black theologians can make a better case for contemporary black theology as a distinctive phenomenon, or as something quite different from white Western theology. Steps in this direction are now being taken by the black theologians Will Coleman and Dwight N. Hopkins, but their conclusions about African sacred beliefs and their significance for shaping a black liberation theology are heavily marred by a serious lack of spadework in African traditions.[3]

Chapter two examines the themes of hope and liberation in the teachings and practices of the black church and the black preacher during slavery, contending that this should serve as a foundation and point of departure for any contemporary theology that speaks to the historic realities of black life in America. In other words, black theologians do not have to look, as some have done over the last three decades, to Jurgen Moltman's *Theology of Hope* (1965) and Ruhem A. Alves's *A Theology of Human Hope* (1972) for categories in an effort to shape a black liberation theology. A much more legitimate source is afforded in the oral traditions of the black church and the black preacher, which found their most powerful expression in antebellum America in prayers, sermons, songs, and tales.

The third chapter covers the visions of God projected by black churches and preachers from 1865 to 1968 as they responded to the range of spiritual, social, psychological, intellectual, economic, and political challenges confronting their people. The dates for the beginning and ending of this discussion coincide with that period stemming from Reconstruction to the assassination of Martin Luther King, Jr. and the climax of the most explosive phase of the modern civil rights movement. Black preachers from Daniel J. Russell in the late nineteenth century to Martin Luther King, Jr in the mid-twentieth century are treated in terms of the ideas of God they set forth in the struggle for black liberation and survival, and some attention is given to the importance of those ideas for black theology today. Black churches and preachers are placed in four categories -- pietistic perfectionism, progressive accommodationism, prophetic pragmatism, and religious nationalism – and representatives of these traditions are highlighted in terms of how their theologies and praxis related to the poor and the oppressed.[4]

Chapter four focuses on the historic struggles of African American women to find full acceptance as preachers and pastors in black churches. From Jarena Lee in the antebellum period to contemporary figures like Ella P. Mitchell and Bernice A. King, African American female preachers have challenged the policies of gender-exclusiveness that have always characterized ministry and leadership in the black church. The black theologian James H. Cone, echoing the thoughts of many black womanist theologians, feels that the issue of women in ministry will be one of the greatest challenges confronting the black church in the twenty- first century.[5] This prediction cannot be logically denied. Equally important are the implications of this issue for the shaping of a black liberation theology and ethic. This work holds that the ideal of "the gender-inclusive church," so long advocated by African American females in ministry, must be taken more seriously by black theology if it is to claim its rightful place in the broad field of liberation thought.

Chapter five consists of personal reflections on how the black church, black preachers, and black theology might become more relevant for African Americans today and in the future. The contention is that they must become more involved in the daily concerns and issues that impact the quality of black life, ranging from crime, gang activity, and teenage pregnancy to racism, sexism, and economic justice. Too many black churches and their leaders are confining their ministry and missions within their own consecrated walls, and are failing to make them relevant to the needs of African Americans in general. Moreover, black theologians are not taking seriously the raw data provided by sociologists and other social scientists on problems in the African American community, and this explains why their theological reflections do not touch base with mass culture.

This book is a constructive critique of contemporary black liberation theology. While recognizing some of the strengths of this phenomenon as an expression of African American attitudes toward God and God's role in human experience, it is devoted more to the need for a reconstruction of black theology. That process must occur not only at the level of sources, but also with reference to categories and models for doing theology. This conviction is grounded in my more than two decades of ministry to African Americans in the church, the academy, and the military.

The larger questions at issue here are: Where do we go from here? How can the traditions of the black church and the black preacher be made more relevant to the black theological task? Must black theology continue to find its primary locus in the academy, or should it seek better avenues for linking itself to the proximate and ultimate concerns of local black church constituents and the African American community as a whole? How can the multitude of black problems be sufficiently addressed through black church praxis and black theological discourse? The answers to these and other questions will come when we fully realize that our work in the church and as theologians cannot be separated from the world that surrounds us. The common view that the church must separate itself from the world, and that theology has little if anything to do with persons who are untutored and unchurched, must be totally abandoned. If we truly believe that God so loved the world that God sacrificed Self for its salvation, and if we are convinced that theology from the bottom up is as authentic as that from the top down, then there are no other options aside from radical involvement in the totality of human life.

Nevalon Mitchell, Jr.
Bowie, Maryland
March 2004

Notes

1. Only a few black preachers and pastors have produced important critical works on black liberation theology, among which are R. L. Jordan, *Black Theology Exposed* (New York: Vantage Press, 1982), pp. 1-87; Amos Jones, Jr., *Paul's Message of Freedom: What Does it Mean to the Black Church?* (Valley Forge, Pa.: Judson Press, 1984), pp. 11-226; and James H. Harris, *Pastoral Theology: A Black-Church Perspective* (Minneapolis: Fortress Press, 1991), pp. 3-129.

2. Although Cecil Cone identifies this problem in black liberation theology, he does not sufficiently explain how it might be corrected through a more serious engagement of black mass culture, and particularly the traditions of the black church and the black preacher. See Cecil W. Cone, *The Identity Crisis in Black Theology* (Nashville: The African Methodist Episcopal Church, 1975), pp. 15-144. In his first book, James Cone quoted more nom Karl Barth and Dietrich Bonhoeffer than he did from the slave preachers. See James H. Cone, *Black Theology and Black Power* (New York: The Seabury Press, 1969), pp. 1-152.

3. See Coleman's and Hopkins's essays in Dwight N. Hopkins and George C. L. Cummings, ed., *Cut Loose Your Stammering Tongue: Black Theology in the Slave Narratives* (Maryknoll, N.Y.: Orbis Books, 1991), pp. 1-45 and 67-102.

4. These categories have developed out of my reading of Robert M. Franklin, "Religious Belief and Political Activism in Black America: An Essay," *The Journal of Religious Thought*, 43, no. 2 (Fall-Winter, 1986-87), pp. 63-72; and Lewis V. Baldwin, *To Make the Wounded Whole: The Cultural Legacy of Martin Luther King. Jr.* (Minneapolis: Fortress Press, 1992), pp. 7-55.

5. See James H. Cone, *For My People -- Black Theology and the Black Church: Where Have We Been and Where are We Going?* (Maryknoll, N.Y.: Orbis Books, 1984), pp. 122-139 and 203204.

Chapter One

The Black Church and the Black Preacher: African Roots

Hail! all hail! ye Afric clan
Hail! ye oppressed, ye Afric band
Who toil and sweat in slavery bound
When your health and strength are gone
And left no hunger and to mourn.
Let *Independence* be your aim,
Ever mindful what 'tis worth.
Pledge your bodies for the prize
Pile them even to the skies.

Slave Song

On almost every large plantation, and
in every neighborhood of small ones,
there is one man who has come to be
considered the head or pastor of the
local church. The office among the
Negroes, as among all other people,
confers a certain importance and power.

Frederick Olmsted[2]

The African roots of black culture in the United States have been the subject of much discussion and debate. Three basic positions have emerged on the subject over time. One is that the Africans enslaved in America were devoid of culture, and, therefore, had no cultural foundation on which to build in the New

World.[3] Another is that while Africans were torn from vital and sophisticated cultures in their tribal villages, those cultures were virtually destroyed as they were subjected to a brutal slave system and transformed by exposure to a more a dominant Euro-American culture.[4] Yet another view is that powerful remnants of African cultures survived in the New World and figured prominently in the shaping of both American culture and a distinct African American culture.[5]

This chapter assumes the validity of this third position, especially in relation to African American religion and the whole realm of spiritual values. It shows how African cultural elements and values contributed to the shaping of the traditions of the black church and the black preacher. It also establishes the tremendous importance of these traditions for fashioning an authentic black theology, and concludes that that theology will remain deficient as long as it fails to take seriously the history and traditions of the black church and the black preacher. This chapter adds yet another dimension to the continuing scholarship on black theology as both an intellectual discipline and an expression of African American oral culture.[6]

African American Religion in Context: African Traditions and the Rise of the Black Church

Numerous tribes were represented among the Africans who were forcibly brought to America in the two centuries prior to the Civil War. Taken primarily from parts of West and Central Africa, they included the Bambara, Fulani, Hausa, Mandinke, Serer, and Wolof. These tribes came with their own religious traditions, which formed much of the foundation for religious institutions they developed on these shores. W. E. B. DuBois was the first scholar to give due recognition to these developments, noting, in his classic study, *The Negro Church* (1903), that the black church and the black preacher were extensions of African tribal traditions:

> The Negro Church was the only social institution among the Negroes which started in the African forest and survived slavery, and under the priest and medicine man preserved the remnants of African tribal life.[7]

DuBois was equally assertive and forthright in another statement, insisting that the slave church was essentially <u>African</u> before it assumed Christian elements through exposure to Euro-American missionary culture:

> It was not at first by any means a Christian Church, but a mere adaptation of those heathen rites which we roughly designate by the term Obe worship, or "Voodooism. Association and missionary effort soon gave these rites a veneer of Christianity, and gradually, after two centuries, the Church became Christian, with a simple Calvinistic creed, but with many of the old customs still clinging to the services.[8]

DuBois' claims about continuity between African tribal practices and the rise of the black preacher and the black church in America have not met with full acceptance in scholarly circles. Such claims are nevertheless persuasive and quite difficult to refute, particularly since the earliest African imports were adults steeped in their native traditions and consumed with a desire to continue those traditions in one form or another in their new environments.

The black church reflected Africa in so many ways from its origins. As early as the mid-eighteenth century, it became the vehicle through which an essentially <u>African</u> sense of the <u>spiritual</u> found expression in the United States. The church was rooted in the African idea that spirits pervade the universe, and that the sacred and secular are inseparable entities. Moreover, the church nurtured the African conception of the supernatural, and of the connection between transcendent spiritual reality and natural social reality, even as African slaves struggled in a white Western society that separated the natural and the supernatural, the spiritual from the material, and the sacred from the profane.[9]

The prominence of the church in African American life during slavery mirrored what had been the pervasiveness of tribal religious values and customs in the lives of Africans on the continent. The church was linked to every aspect of black life, including the religious, the social, the political, the recreational, and the intellectual, thus establishing itself as "an all-comprehending institution."[10] Tribal religions in Africa had assumed the same central place in the lives of natives. DuBois undoubtedly had this in mind when he asserted the links between the slave church and African tribal life.

The church also embodied African-based communal values. It became an extended family, an institution that sought to preserve kinship ties and a sense of family and family values even as slavery tore at the seams of black communal existence.[11] Respect for elders in the slave community, a tradition markedly <u>African</u>, continued through black churches, and these institutions honored the sacred domain of the ancestors and those soon to be ancestors.[12] No where was this more evident than in the practice of decorating graves and in the pilgrimages taken by the faithful to the graves of black church pioneers during the slavery period.[13] Here the church evoked memories of the role of the clan among tribes in West and Central Africa.[14]

African practices that carried over through the black church, often in a diluted form, included spirit possession. This practice

was manifested in supreme ways in the shouting and holy dancing that were a part of black church worship styles well into the
twentieth century.[15] Like the ring shout among the Gullah on the
Sea Islands of Georgia and South Carolina, these practices,
referred to as "frenzy" by DuBois, emerged as derivatives of
African spirit possession.[16] The fact that shouting and holy dancing existed on some level in both the antebellum South and North
is a measure of the strength of African cultural patterns in North
America. Melville J. Herskovits and Eugene D. Genovese are a
part of a school of thought that believes that shouting and religious dance among African Americans harked back to Africa.[17]
Their position on the subject finds reinforcement in even a cur-
sory study of the Big Quarterly festival, an annual African
American religious event which began in connection with the
African Union Church in Wilmington, Delaware in 1813, and
which drew slaves and free Africans from as far South as
Maryland and as far North as New York. African steps and motor
behavior were also revealed in the shouting and dancing at the
festival, often extending out of black churches into the streets of
Wilmington. The following account of the shout at the 1882 festival brings to mind ceremonies so typical even today of blacks
on the Gullah Islands, who have remained closer to Africa than
African Americans in most parts of the United States:

> Here the most powerful singers and shouters took pos-
> session of the center of the floor, drew their coats and got
> right down to business in a short time. They sang simple
> and oft-repeated octuplets, dwelling with all the strength
> of their voices in the chorus, slapping their hands
> together, stomping their feet and jumping up and down
> for half an hour at a stretch; while all around the church
> men and women, catching the infection, would join in
> the jumping and shouting and swing their arms around

convulsively, while the shrieks of penitents and the hallelujahs of the saints joined to swell the sound until it became one complete and overpowering mass of voice. Then someone in the circle of exhausted shouters would swing his arms upward and breathlessly cry out: "Brethren, let's go down now," and the singing would give way to a short session of equally earnest prayer.[18]

Also revealing is the report concerning religious dance at the 1883 Big Quarterly, where images of Africa surfaced with unmistakable clarity and power:

In the basement of the church a hundred or more men formed a circle and swayed to and fro, sometimes fast and sometimes slow, according to the metre of the hymn sung. Those who formed the inner line of the human ring were the most violent in their movements and most of the time perspired so freely that they could not have been more wet if a hose had been turned upon them. Frantically, they urged one another to more violent feats of gymnastic devotion, clapping their hands, jumping and shouting, and occasionally groaning. When they grew weary they dropped upon their knees and prayers were offered. The women were modest and did not help form the rings. Instead they sang and watched the proceedings with interest.[19]

Such displays of religious power and emotional exuberance, during which shouting and singing merged with the chanting, groaning, and praying in ways that sent the average slave into ecstasy, would have been understood and claimed by blacks anywhere in Africa and the diaspora. Clearly, the black church in the nineteenth century was far more *African* in character than even some of the most ardent proponents of this view have suggested.[20]

Much of the singing in early black churches derived in manner from Africa.[21] The call-and-response pattern which characterized slave songs in the church illustrates this point. A slave leader, most commonly a preacher, was known to recite lyrics from hymns, after which the congregation joined together in the singing of those lyrics, thus creating exchanges between the leader and the other congregants that recalled the folk sermon. This "lining out of hymns," as it was called, united speech and singing with bodily movement, reflecting African customs centuries old.

Lawrence W. Levine has noted that the style of singing among the slaves, with its over-riding antiphony, its group nature, its pervasive functionality, its improvisational character, its strong relationship in performance to dance and bodily movement and expression, remained closer to the musical styles and performances of West Africa and the Afro-American Music of the West Indies and South America than to the musical style of Western Europe.[22]

This view was also held by DuBois, who declared that slave songs "sprung from the African forests...."[23] DuBois further noted how the sacred songs of the slaves, much like those of Africa, grew out of and reflected the circumstances of daily life. He explained how slave music was "adapted, changed, and intensified by the tragic soul-life of the slave, until, under the stress of law and whip, it became the one true expression of a people's sorrow, despair, and hope."[24] This point has strong implications for any study of how African traditions were transformed to meet the spiritual needs of Africans in the New World.

Burial practices that emerged very early in black churches afforded some of the most glaring proof of African retentions. Wakes, shallow burials, the passing of small children over or underneath the coffin, the inclusion of food and personal effects in the coffin, and grave decorations were a common feature of religion, particularly as it developed in the slave quarters and in the invisible institution.[25] This mortuary art, or what Robert Farris Thompson terms "art for the dead," has long been typical of Africans and their descendants, thus bridging the gap between the spiritual and the material in ways untypical of the Europeans who enslaved them.[26]

Religion among early African imports was life, and it most certainly embraced attitudes toward death as well. Death was perceived not so much as the end of life, but as an extension of life in a different form. This view became a central part of early black church theology. The idea of death as a higher and more lasting stage of life was revealed to some extent in the notion of surviving spirits. The spirits of the ancestors, it was believed, continued to live among those who lived and functioned on earth.[27] This explains why slaves, much like Africans thousands of years before them, visited the graves of ancestors seeking advice on critical life questions and decisions. The belief was that the spirits of the dead could either enhance or diminish the quality of life for surviving relatives and friends, depending on the levels of respect shown by the living for such spirits.[28]

The point at which the black church became more "American" than "African" cannot be determined with precision. W. E. B. DuBois suggests that this transition had occurred for the most part by 1750, as slaves surrendered their own essentially African religious values and systems in favor of a new and more Christian philosophy of life:

By the middle of the eighteenth century the black slave had sunk, with hushed murmurs, to his place at the bottom

24

of a new economic system, and was unconsciously ripe for
a new philosophy of life. Nothing suited his condition better than the doctrines of passive submission embodied in
the newly learned Christianity.... Courtesy became humil-
ity, moral strength degenerated into submission, and the
exquisite native appreciation of the beautiful became an
infinite capacity for dumb suffering. The Negro, losing the
joy of this world, eagerly seized upon the offered conceptions of the next; the avenging spirit of the Lord enjoining
patience in this world, under sorrow and tribulation until
the Great Day when He shall lead His dark children home,
-- this became his comforting dream.[29]

While underscoring the gradual impact of Western Christianity
on African slaves, DuBois, at the same time, concludes that the
black church in its most developed state was neither completely
"American" nor completely "African." Rather, it was a hybrid that
combined both "Christian" and "African" elements.[30]

Throughout the first half of the nineteenth century, the
power of Africa was reflected not only in the styles and ethos of
black churches, but also in their liberation theology. Even as
African Americans spoke and sang of the love and servant-hood
of Jesus Christ, they maintained a keen sense of intimacy with
the deity that called to mind African traditions and that freed the
outcast and the enslaved. As Lawrence W. Levine puts it, "The
God the slaves sang of was neither remote nor abstract, but as
intimate, personal, and immediate as the gods of Africa had
been."[31] With an essentially African view of how the deity relates
to humans, African Americans were not likely to subscribe to the
commonly Western notion of a transcendent God who is oblivious to human affairs.

The image of Africa was prominently evident in the theological reflections of early nineteenth century writers such as Robert

A. Young and David Walker, both of whom had ties with the black church. Gayraud S. Wilmore attributes to Young, the author of *The Ethiopian Manifesto* (1829), "a deep-lying African spirituality" and "a kind of God-Madness" that gave early black theology its most prophetic edge.[32] Emerging out of Walker's *Appeal* (1829) is a sense of a strong warrior God that rivals in power and presence the personal <u>chi</u> of any nineteenth century Ibo villager.[33] Such conceptions of God were influenced by African ideas concerning the divine, and they challenge the notion that early black theology was merely otherworldly and escapist in character.

The Black Preacher and the Folk Sermon: Art in the Service of Freedom

The rise of the black preacher in America must be understood in relation to Africa. The earliest religious leaders among the slaves on the plantations, according to DuBois and Melville J. Herskovits, were priests and medicine men from West Africa.[34] In fact, the power and function of African priests, medicine men, and ritual elders became that of the slave preacher as well, because the preacher in the slave quarters also drew on African values in helping his people to deal spiritually and emotionally with the pain of bondage.

Euro-American standards are insufficient to capture the image and roles of the earliest religious leaders among the slaves, mainly because the priesthood in African tribal societies included males and females. African priests and priestesses wielded great influence, as evidenced by the fact that only such figures could enter the temple in many tribal societies. Laity were typically confined to the compounds outside the temple.[35] The power of the priesthood in Africa extended far beyond what Westerners would have termed the spiritual and the ecclesiastical to embrace the social and political. Priests were so often both religious and tribal political leaders. Moreover, they embodied the most vital of the spiritual and artistic in their African villages, prefiguring the slave preacher on American soil.

The presence of African priests and medicine men on the plantations contributed to an early process of Pan-Africanization. Portraying the slave preacher as an agent of Pan-Africanization, James Weldon Johnson, building on the conclusions of DuBois, notes that this figure united various tribal groups among the slaves around a common bond of identity and solidarity:

> It was through him that the people of diverse languages and customs who were brought here from diverse parts of Africa and thrown into slavery were given their first sense of unity and solidarity. He was the first shepherd of this bewildered flock.[36]

This image of the earliest preachers among the slaves is borne out in the writings of Charles Hamilton, H. Beecher Hicks, Jr., and Sterling Stuckey. Hamilton's portrait of the slave preacher as "a linkage figure" and Hicks' view of that personality as "a unifying influence" are self-explanatory. Stuckey describes the slave preacher as one steeped in African consciousness and values, qualities which made him the primary influence in helping the slaves to transcend African ethnicity in the interest of black unity in America. Stuckey writes in poignant terms about DuBois' view that the slave "priest's presence in the church represented one African institution within another," and about James Weldon Johnson's thesis that "the mediating influence of the old Negro preacher helped African ethnic groups find commonality."[37]

As was the case with spiritual leaders in Africa, the slave preacher in America performed a multitude of functions which united the sacred and the secular. He was a religious leader as well as a political figure, an authoritarian and a servant, a thinker as well as an artist of unmistakable genius. W. E. B. DuBois underscored these qualities as part of the uniqueness of the black preacher and of the black preaching tradition.

> The preacher is the most unique personality developed by the Negro on American soil. A leader, a politician, an orator, a "boss," an intriguer, an idealist, -- all these he is, and ever, too, the centre of a group of men, now twenty, now a thousand in number.[38]

In *Roll, Jordan, Roll*, Eugene D. Genovese explains how the religious leaders among the slaves embodied the attributes of the preacher, exhorter, and conjurer. The preacher was one who majored in the proclamation of the Word of God. The exhorter was one who often preached without the blessings of the master or the institutional confirmation of the white church. The conjurer was a spiritual leader who could draw on the powers of the divine and of nature for the purpose of healing, interpreting the supernatural, or bringing good or ill to others through the use of magic. The fact that some slave preachers personified all three of these elements suggests something more about the African background as a force in the shaping of slave religious culture.[39] This threefold function cast the slave preacher in the mold of the African priest, who, in the words of Benjamin C. Ray, "mediated the sacred to the people."[40] Sterling Stuckey had the same in mind when he identified the slave preacher as one who mediated "between the living and the dead, in order to prevent or lessen the hardship for the living."[41]

The male preachers were not the only ones who embodied these elements. Reflecting traditions deeply grounded in African tribal cultures, a slave woman named Sinda attained considerable influence as a prophetess on her Georgia plantation because of her powers to tell fortunes and predict the future. Such capacities were typical of both males and females who assumed spiritual leadership among their people. On the Georgia Sea Islands, an old African woman called Maum Katie, who remembered "worshipping her own gods in Africa," fulfilled functions of this nature. Such African women were able to combine the gift of preaching with the wisdom and skill of the conjurer, thereby reflecting the power and durability of the African heritage.[42] They stirred memories of African tribal societies in which women oversaw temples, prayed, led in public worship, and acted as seers, mediums, and fortune tellers.[43]

The power of both slave men and women as spiritual leaders came not merely from their roots in African traditions, but also from their claim of having a special relationship with the deity through some type of religious experience. The claim of being called by God meant much more to the slave community than any license or ordination the church might have provided. In other words, charismatic authority was more important than any authority that could have come through the institutional church.[44] Religious leaders among the slaves established their authority by harking back to some kind of transforming encounter with God. African influences on the slave preacher became clearly observable in the development of the folk sermon as a work of art. Here the preacher achieved a high level of skill in his employment of oral traditions, much like the priest and griot in traditional African societies. The preacher became a master storyteller, often singing or chanting his message, recalling the African practice of singing everything communicable to the people.[45] James Weldon Johnson captured the communicative ability of the slave preacher in terms compelling enough to merit extended quotation:

He knew the secret of oratory, that at bottom it is a progression of rhythmic words more than anything else.

Indeed, I have witnessed congregations moved to ecstasy by the rhythmic intoning of sheer incoherences. He was a master of all the modes of eloquence. He often possessed a voice that was a marvelous instrument, a voice he could modulate from a sepulchral whisper to a crashing thunder clap. His discourse was generally kept at a high pitch of fervency, but occasionally he dropped into colloquialisms and, less often, into humor. He preached a personal and anthropomorphic God, a sure -- enough heaven and a red-hot hell. His imagination was bold and unfettered. He had the power to sweep his hearers before him: and so himself was often swept away. At such times his language was not prose but poetry.[46]

Here Johnson captured the full range of the slave preacher's gifts and talents, underscoring his oratorical skills, his marvelous ability to "whoop" or "tune up," his adeptness in the use of imagery, his simplistic message of sin and salvation, and his capacity to appeal to the emotions of his hearers. Johnson may well have had in mind John Jasper, who was for fifty years a slave in Virginia, who was "a beautiful storyteller," and who often "made the house ring" with his hearers' "laughter and with their Shouts."[47]

The folk sermon also assumed much of the call-and-response pattern so characteristic of singing in both African societies and slave culture in the New World. Typically, the slaves responded to the preacher with shouts of "amen," "hallelujah," "preach the word," exchanges that marked the sermon as a collective or communal experience. Communal exchange and participation, so essential in African artistic expression, became as important in the sermon as they were in the songs of the slaves. Frederika Bremer saw this while listening to the responses of blacks to their preacher in 1850, and she reported that "The whole congregation was for several minutes like a stormy sea."[48] Clearly, the folk sermon developed as dialogue and not monologue, and its dialogical character illustrates the degree to which slaves acted out of their own, autonomous religious values.[49]

The fact that the preacher customarily combined body and soul in the delivery of the sermon is further revealing of African influences. As with singing, preaching on the part of slaves was always accompanied by bodily movement and powerful gestures. Preaching as both the spoken word and the performed art was usually inseparable from religious dance and the shout. Even a casual study of the styles of slave preachers like Harry "Black Harry" Hoosier and John Jasper substantiates this observation.[50] The manner in which Jasper injected his entire being into his sermons excited the imagination beyond description, for "the pulpit was the stage of his chief performance":

> Hardly a word came out clothed and in its right mind.
> And gestures! He circled around the pulpit with his ankle
> in his hand; and laughed and sang and shouted and acted
> about a dozen characters within the space of three min-
> utes. Meanwhile, in spite of these things, he was pouring
> out a gospel sermon, red hot, full of love, full of invec-
> tive, full of tenderness, full of bitterness, full of tears, full
> of every passion that ever flamed in the human breast. He
> was a theatre within himself; with the stage crowded
> with actors.[51]

The slave preacher's mastery of the sermon as the spoken word carried reminders of the African priest's skill in oral communication. E. Franklin Frazier once observed that as a communicator of the word, the preacher had to possess some knowledge of scripture, even if he lacked education. Knowledge in this regard necessarily involved the ability to relate the word as revealed in the

Bible to the existential realities of the slaves. Slave preachers were quite adept at emphasizing slavery in Egypt, the Exodus, the experiences of the Israelites in the wilderness, Jesus' identification with outsiders, and other great Biblical themes as historical occurrences that paralleled the black experience. Frederika Bremer wrote graphically of the black preacher who "drew a very ingenious parallel between the captivity of the Israelites in Egypt and the Negroes in America" in a sermon in 1850, thus recalling a tendency that was also common in slave songs.[52]

The multiplicity of roles which connected the slave preacher to the spiritual leader in African tribal traditions cry out for further exploration. More rich and extensive scholarship in this area will show why slave preachers emerged as pivotal figures in the spiritual and material lives of their people. Furthermore, such scholarship should reveal how slave-preachers, despite the handicaps imposed upon them by bondage, became both the embodiment and exemplars of a distinctive African American culture.

The Black Church and Preaching Traditions: Sources for a Viable Liberation Theology

Black theologians have not devoted sufficient attention to the traditions of the black church and the black preacher, particularly as they relate to Africa. This pattern of neglect is part of what Cecil W. Cone would call "the identity crisis in black theology."[53] Like the white theologians they have so freely criticized, black theologians have shaped their discourse as if the African heritage is insignificant. They have not made serious use of the findings of anthropologists, sociologists, and historians on the question of African survivals in slave religion, a tendency quite disturbing since such scholars provide so much of the raw data on which black theologians must reflect in order to be true to their discipline. Black theology emerged as an intellectual discipline in the

United States in the mid-1960s. Black clergy and seminary professors were among its earliest creators and proponents. From its beginnings, black theology demonstrated an inability to divorce itself from the powerful influences of white Western intellectual traditions, even as the relevance of those traditions were called into question by black theologians. James H. Cone, who produced the first book-length manuscript on black theology, seemed more concerned about legitimizing his own ideas with quotations from Karl Barth and Paul Tillich, than with providing a serious treatment of how the traditions of the black church and the black preacher could inform a viable liberation theology within the African American context.[54] Trained in white seminaries and graduate schools, where the African roots of black Americans were not taken seriously, Cone, J. Deotis Roberts, Major Jones, and other black theologians were ill-prepared to treat slave religion and culture as primary sources for their theological reflections.

While claiming to make the black experience the point of departure for doing theology, Cone, Roberts, and others virtually ignored W. E. B. DuBois' and Melville J. Herskovits' insistence that one has to look to Africa in order to understand many of the traditions embodied in the black church and the black preacher.[55] Like white theologians, these shapers of the new black theology assumed that because slavery stripped blacks of so much of their African heritage, there was no need to give serious attention to the findings of DuBois and Herskovits. Moreover, they refused to offer a strong challenge to E. Franklin Frazier's conclusions regarding the complete destruction of the African cultural heritage.[56] This same tendency is reflected in the writings of Albert B. Cleage, Jr., the black Christian nationalist and theologian, who challenges his people to recapture a strong sense of their identity as it relates to Africa and African modes of thinking and viewing the world.[57]

This ambivalent character of black theology rendered it suspect from the very beginning, for it affirmed blackness and the black experience without coming to terms with that which made African Americans unique and different from other peoples in America. The maturation of black theology through the 1970s, the 1980s, and the early 1990s did not alter this tendency, despite the emergence of more recent scholarship which affirmed the impact of Africanisms on American religion, music, and aesthetics.[58]

Black womanist ethicists and theologians such as Jacquelyn Grant and Katie G. Cannon made the historic experiences of black women the norm for articulating their ideas about God and human liberation, but they, like black male theologians, virtually ignored the scholarship on the whole question of African retentions in black religion and culture.[59] The same applies in the case of more recent womanist thinkers like Delores S. Williams, Kelly Brown Douglas, and Cheryl J. Sanders, despite their efforts to relate womanism to developing trends in Afrocentricity.[60] But there is hope for the further development of black theology in the recognition by womanists that African identity, loyalty, and values are essential for doing theology in the African American context.[61]

Will Coleman and Dwight N. Hopkins are exceptions in this tendency among black theologians to undermine the importance of the African background of the slaves for contemporary theological reflection on the black experience. Coleman explores the roles of priests, priestess, conjurers, and early preachers and prophets among the slaves as mediators of the sacred, building on a perspective set forth by W. E. B. DuBois, James Weldon Johnson, and Sterling Stuckey.[62] Hopkins gives attention to the ways in which African sacred beliefs, or notions of God and the universe, merged with Euro-American Christian values to shape an Afro-Christian theology among the slaves.[63]

The failure of much of black theology to adequately consider the image of Africa in the shaping of the traditions of the black church and the black preacher further illustrates the chasms that have existed since the 1960s between what black theologians are writing and what the masses of African Americans believe and practice. In order to be true to themselves and to the traditions they claim, black theologians must break with the intellectual standards that have sought to understand African Americans devoid of their ancestral roots in Africa.[64] This need is all the more significant because African Americans are not, and never have been, mere carbon copies of white Americans.

Two concerns must become perennially important as black theologians seek to arrive at a theology that speaks authentically to black traditions, and that is truly liberating for the bodies, minds, and spirits of African Americans. First, they must take seriously the slaves' memories of Africa and the part that African values played in meeting their psychological, social, and spiritual needs, and in the shaping of their religious institutions and practices. Second, black theologians must become more sensitive to the ways in which African traditions and values interacted with those of Euro-Americans to create a distinctive African American perspective and culture. This is most certainly one of the greatest challenges facing black theologians in the future. Such a challenge can be met if black theologians take seriously anthropological, sociological, and historical studies of black cultural forms from slavery times to the present. The employment of various disciplines, singly and in clusters, to interpret the traditions of the black church and the black preacher will enable them to answer more thoroughly one of the most perplexing questions confronting them: What is the meaning of God in light of the black experience of oppression and victimization? Until theological reconstruction occurs along these lines, Christian theology will have little meaning for African Americans.

Endnotes

1. Quoted in Sterling Stuckey, ed., *The Ideological Origins of Black Nationalism* (Boston: Beacon Press, 1972), p. 4.

2. Frederick Law Olmsted, *A Journey in the Seaboard Slave States* (1856; reprinted in New York, 1969), p. 450.

3. Matthew Estes, *A Defense of Negro Slavery, as it Exists in the United States* (Montgomery, Ala.: Press of the Alabama Journal, 1846), pp. 49-95; and Ulrich B. Phillips, *American Negro Slavery* (Baton Rouge, La.: Louisiana State University Press, 1966), pp. xix, 309-330, and 425-488.

4. E. Franklin Frazier, *The Negro Church in America* (New York: Schocken books, 1963), pp. 1-19.

5. Melville J. Herskovits, *The Myth of the Negro Past* (Boston: Beacon Press, 1990; originally published in 1941), pp. 1-299; Leonard E. Barrett, *Soul-Force: African Heritage in Afro-American Religion* (New York: Doubleday & Company, Inc., 1974), pp. 13-39; Gwendolyn Midlo Hall, *Africans in Colonial Louisiana: The Development of Afro-Creole Culture in the Eighteenth Century* (Baton Rouge, La.: Louisiana State University Press, 1992), pp. 2 and 158-159; Lawrence W. Levine, *Black Culture and Black Consciousness: Afro-American Folk Thought from Slavery to Freedom* (New York: Oxford University Press, 1977), pp. ix-xiv; Sterling Stuckey, *Slave Culture: Nationalist Theory and the Foundations of Black America* (New York: Oxford University Press, 1987), pp. vii-x and 3-97; David Roediger, The Meaning of Africa for the American Slave," *The Journal of Ethnic Studies*, 4, no. 4 (Winter, 1977), pp. 1-15; and Margaret Washington Creel, ?A Peculiar People": Slave Religion and Community-Culture Among the Gullahs* (New York: New York University Press, 1988), pp. 29-63. The most impressive treatment of African influences on both black and white cultures in the United States is Joseph E. Holloway, ed., *Africanisms in American Culture* (Bloomigton and Indianapolis: Indiana University Press, 1990), pp. 1-237.

6. The African roots of the slave preacher has not been studied seriously. The most important references to the subject are found in the writings of W. E. B. DuBois, James Weldon Johnson, and Sterling Stuckey. See John Hope Franklin, ed., *The Souls of Black Folk in Three Negro Classics* (New York: Avon Books, 1965), p. 342; James Weldon Johnson, *God's Trombones: Seven Negro Sermons in Verse*

(New York: The Viking Press, 1927), p. 2; and Stuckey, *Slave Culture*, pp. 255-257.

7. W. E. B. DuBois, *The Negro Church: A Social Study Done Under the Direction of Atlanta University* (Atlanta: Atlanta University Press, 1903), p. 2; and W. E. B. DuBois, *Some Efforts of the American Negroes for Their Own Betterment* (Atlanta: Atlanta University Press, 1898), pp. 1-5.

8. DuBois, *Some Efforts of the American Negroes for Their Own Betterment*, pp. 1-2. DuBois's conclusion is supported by the findings in Stuckey, *Slave Culture*, pp. 256-257.

9. These conclusions are corroborated by the findings in Levine, *Black Culture and Black Consciousness*, pp. 3-135; and Stuckey, *Slave Culture*, pp. 3-97. An interesting discussion of how transcendent spiritual reality combined with natural social reality in the conversion experiences of slaves is found in Edward P. Wimberly and Anne S. Wimberly, *Liberation & Human Wholeness: The Conversion Experiences of Black People in Slavery & Freedom* (Nashville: Abingdon Press, 1986), pp. 14-23.

10. The term "all-comprehending institution" was initially used in Carter G. Woodson, "*The Negro Church*, an All-Comprehending Institution," *The Negro History Bulletin*, III, no. 1 (October, 1939), p. 7. For further discussion of the term, see Milton C. Sernett, *Black Religion and American Evangelicalism: White Protestants, Plantation Missions, and the Flowering of Negro Christianity, 1787-1865* (Metuchen, N.J.: Scarecrow Press, 1975)m p, 19.

11. This subject has not been treated sufficiently by scholars. Exceptions are Wallace C. Smith, *The Church in the Life of the Black Family* (Valley Forge, Pa.: Judson Press, 1985), pp. 13-111; J. Deotis Roberts, Sr., "A Black Ecclesiology of Involvement," *The Journal of Religious Thought*, XXXII, no. 1 (Spring-Summer, 1975), pp. 40-41; and J. Deotis Roberts, Sr., *Roots of a Black Future: Family and Church* (Philadelphia: The Westminster Press, 1980), pp. 57-79.

12. This view finds reinforcement in Stuckey, *Slave Culture*, pp. 333-334.

13. See Robert F. Thompson, *flash of the Spirit: African and Afro-American Art & Philosophy* (New York: Vintage Books, 1983), pp. 109-157; and Lewis V. Baldwin, *"Invisible" Strands in African Methodism: A History of the African Union Methodist Protestant and Union American Methodist Episcopal Churches,*

1805-1980 (Metuchen, N.J.: Scarecrow Press, 1983), pp. 144-146 and 239-241.

14. This topic still awaits serious exploration, even by scholars who have examined the relationship between church and family in African American culture. For insights into the workings of the clan in African tribal life, insights that are useful for making comparisons between the clan and the slave church, see Chinua Achebe, *Things Fall Apart* (New York: Anchor Books/Doubleday, 1959), pp. 1-103.

15. The African roots of the shout and religious dance, and their links to African spirit possession, are explored in Stuckey, *Slave Culture*, pp. viii-ix and 10-17. One source which distinguishes the shout from the holy dance, but fails to connect either with African traditions, is Clifton H. Johnson, ed., *God Struck Me Dead: Voices of Ex-Slaves* (Cleveland: The Pilgrim Press, 1993; originally published in 1969), pp. 10-12.

16. Franklin, ed., *The Souls of Black Folk in Three Negro Classics*, p. 338.

17. Herskovits, *The Myth of the Negro Past*, pp. 261-281; and Eugene D. Genovese, *Roll, Jordan, Roll: The World the Slaves Made* (New York: Pantheon Books, 1974), pp. 233-234, 238, 240, and 723 n. 31.

18. See Baldwin, *"Invisible" Strand in African Methodism*, p. 137; and *Every Evening*, Wilmington, Delaware (August 28, 1882), p. 1.

19. Baldwin, *"Invisible" Strand in African Methodism*, p. 139; and *The Delaware State Journal*, Wilmington, Delaware (August 30, 1986), p. 1. The white reporters who provided such descriptions clearly viewed blacks in stereotypical terms, but their accounts are still colorful and quit useful for linking African traditions to the black church in the nineteenth century. This concern is dealt with to some degree in Lewis V. Baldwin, "Setting the Record Straight: Wilmington Newspapers and the Big Quarterly Festival, 1840-1986," *Big Quarterly 86* (Chester, Pa.: Linder Printing, 1986), pp. 14-18.

20. This is made abundantly clear in Baldwin, *"Invisible" Strands in African Methodism*, pp. 126-146.

21. Melville J. Herskovits is mentioned in connection with this point in Arthur H. Fauset, *Black Gods of the Metropolis: Negro Religious Cults in the Urban North* (Philadelphia: The University of Pennsylvania Press, 1971), p. 101.

22. Levine, *Black Culture and Black Consciousness*, p. 6.

23. Franklin, ed., *The Souls of Black Folk in Three Negro Classics*, p. 338.

24. *Ibid.*, pp. 338-339.

25. See Fauset, *Black Gods of the Metropolis*, p. 101. The Invisible Institution refers to the clandestine meetings of the slaves ? meetings held in the absence of white slaveowners and overseers. See Frazier, *The Negro Church in America*, pp. 16-19.

26. Thompson, *Flash of the Spirit*, pp. 3-268; and Robert Farris Thompson, "Siras Bowens of Sunbury, Georgia: A Tidewater Artist in the Afro-American Visual Tradition," *The Massachusetts Review*, XVIII, no. 3 (Autumn, 1977), pp. 490-499.

27. Stuckey, *Slave Culture*, pp. 4-7; and Lewis V. Baldwin, "A Home in Dat Rock: Afro-American Folk Sources and Slave Visions of Heaven and Hell," *The Journal of Religious Thought*, 41, no. 1 (Spring-Summer, 1984), pp. 38-57.

28. Baldwin "*A Home in Dat Rock*," pp. 38-57; and Stuckey, *Slave Culture*, pp. 4-9.

29. Franklin, ed., *The Souls of Black folk in Three Negro Classics*, p. 344; and Baldwin, *"Invisible" Strands in African Methodism*, p. 10. DuBois's conclusions regarding the breakdown of African religious values in the slave church is not shared by Sterling Stuckey, who concludes that the constant arrival of slaves from Africa via the slave trade after 1750 reinforces existing Africanisms in the culture. See Stuckey, *Slave Culture*, p. 259.

30. DuBois, *The Negro Church*, p. 2; and Baldwin, *"Invisible" Strands in African Methodism*, p. 10.

31. Levine, *Black Culture and Black Consciousness*, p. 35.

32. Gayraud S. Wilmore, *Black Religion and Black Radicalism: An Interpretation of the Religious History of Afro-American People* (Maryknoll, N.Y.: Orbis books, 1983), p. 36.

33. See Charles M. Wiltse, ed., *David Walker's Appeal. in Four Articles: Together with a Preamble to the Coloured Citizens of the World* (New York: Hill and Wang, 1965; originally published in 1829), pp. 25-30.

34. Franklin, ed., *The Souls of Black Folk in Three Negro Classics*, pp. 338 and 342; and Herskovits, *The Myth of the Negro Past*, pp. 207-260.

35. John S. Mbiti, *Introduction to African Religion* (New York: Praeger Publishers, 1975), pp. 159-161; and Geoffrey Parrinder, *African Traditional Religion* (New York: Harper & Row, Publishers, 1962), p. 19.

36. Johnson, *God's Trombones*, p. 2.

37. Charles V. Hamilton, *The Black Preacher in America* (New York: William Morrow & Company, Inc., 1972), pp. 11-69; H. Beecher Hicks, Jr., *Images of the Black Preacher: The Man Nobody Knows* (Valley Forge, Pa.: Judson Press, 1977), pp. 33-34; and Stuckey, *Slave Culture*, pp. 255-257.

38. Franklin, ed., *The Souls of Black Folk in Three Negro Classics*, p. 338.

39. Genovese, *Roll, Jordan, Roll*, pp. 255-257.

40. Benjamin C. Ray, *African Religions: Symbol, Ritual, and Community* (Englewood Cliffs, N.J.: Prentice-Hall Inc., 1976), p. 17.

41. Stuckey, *Slave Culture*, p. 255.

42. Albert J. Raboteau, *Slave Religion: The "Invisible Institution" in the Antebellum South* (New York: Oxford University Press, 1978), pp. 238-239.

43. Mbiti, *Introduction to African Religion*, pp. 159-161. An important source for locating women in the tradition of the religious leader among the slaves is Cheryl T. Gilkes, "The Politics of 'Silence': Dual-Sex Political Systems and Women's Traditions of Conflict in African-American Religion," in Paul E. Johnson, ed., *African-American Christianity: essays in History* (Berkeley: University of California Press, 1994), pp. 81-85.

44. This view is confirmed by the slaves' accounts of their "calls to preach." For example, see Hatcher's discussion of the experience that the slave preacher John Jasper had with God in William E. Hatcher, *John Jasper: The Unmatched Negro Philosopher and Preacher* (New York: Fleming H. Revell Company, 1908), pp. 23-29.

45. Henry H. Mitchell, *Black Preaching* (Philadelphia: J. B. Lippincott Company, 1970), pp. 65-111.

46. Johnson, *God's Trombones*, p. 5.

47. Hatcher, *John Jasper*, pp. 80 and 82.

48. Quoted in Harold Courlander, *A Treasury of Afro-American Folklore* (New York: Crown Publishers, Inc., 1976), p. 351.

49. For a brilliant discussion of those characteristics that have traditionally marked the black preaching experience, see William R. Jones, "The Art of Preaching from a Black Perspective," an unpublished paper, pp. 8-9. One scholar draws on Jones's discussion of the dialogical character and other characteristics of black folk preaching in treating Martin Luther King, Jr. in the tradition of the slave preacher. See Lewis V. Baldwin, *There is a Balm in Gilead: The Cultural Roots of Martin Luther King, Jr.* (Minneapolis: Fortress Press, 1991), pp. 291-297.

50. See Warren T. Smith, *Harry Hosier: Circuit Rider* (Nashville: The Upper Room, 1981), pp. 21-62; and Hatcher, *John Jasper*, pp. 23-46 and 174-183. Also see Jones, "The Art of Preaching," pp. 7-9.

51. Hatcher, *John Jasper*, pp. 9 and 36.

52. Courlander, *A Treasury of Afro-American Folklore*, pp. 350351. For insights into the use of parallelism in black folk preaching, see Jones, "The Art of Preaching," p. 8.

53. See Cecil W. Cone, *The Identity Crisis in Black Theology* (Nashville: The African Methodist Episcopal Church, 1975), pp. 7-9 and 26-72.

54. See James H. Cone, *Black Theology and Black Power* (New York: The Seabury Press, 1969), pp. 1-152.

55. Cone, Roberts, and Jones claimed that black history, black culture, and the black experience were major sources of their theological reflections, a claim all the more interesting given their neglect of the whole question of African influences on the shaping of the black church and black religion. See James H. Cone, *A Black Theology of Liberation* (Philadelphia and New York: J. B. Lippincott Company, 1970), pp. 53-62; J. Deotis Roberts, *Liberation and Reconciliation: A Black Theology* (Philadelphia: The Westminster Press, 1971), pp. 13-75; J. Deotis Roberts, *A Black Political Theology* (Philadelphia: The Westminster Press, 1974), pp. 47-73; Major J. Jones, Black Awareness: A Theology of Hope (Nashville: Abingdon Press, 1971), pp. 11-56; and Major J. Jones, *Christian Ethics for Black Theology: The Politics of Liberation* (Nashville: Abingdon Press, 1974), pp. 15-98.

56. Cone made only one fleeting reference to DuBois, two to Frazier, and none to Herskovits in his first two books on Black Theology. See Cone, *Black Theology and Black Power*, pp. 21 and 74; and Cone, *A Black Theology of Liberation*, pp. 17-249.57. Albert B. Cleage, Jr., *The Black Messiah* (New York: Sheed and Ward, Inc., 1968), pp. 3-278; and

Albert B. Cleage, Jr., *Black Christian Nationalism: New Directions for the Black Church* (New York: William Morrow & Company, Inc., 1972), pp. 3-310.

58. See Alfloyd Butler, *The Africanization of American Christianity* (New York: Carlton Press, Inc., 1980), pp. 11-143; Ulysses D. Jenkins, *Ancient African Religion and the African-American Church* (Jacksonville, N.C.: Flame International, 1978), pp. 1-153; Baldwin, *"Invisible" Strands in African Methodism*, pp. 126-146 and 213-241; Holloway, ed., *Africanisms in American Culture*, pp. ix-237; and Stuckey, *Slave Culture*, pp. vii-97.

59. See Jacquelyn Grant, *White Women's Christ and Black Women's Jesus: Feminist Theology and Womanist Response* (Atlanta: Scholars Press, 1989), pp. 9-48; and Katie G. Cannon, *Black Womanist Ethics* (Atlanta: Scholars Press, 1988), pp. 31-104.

60. Afrocentricity means, literally, "placing African ideals at the center of any analysis that involves African culture and behavior." See Molefi Kete Asante, *The Afrocentric Idea* (Philadelphia: Temple University Press, 1987), p.6; and Cheryl J. Sanders, ed., *Living the Intersection: Womanism and Afrocentrism in Theology* (Minneapolis: Fortress Press, 1995), pp. 43-56, 67-77, and 121-143.

61. Sanders, ed., *Living the Intersection*, pp. 9-175.

62. Dwight N. Hopkins and George Cummings, eds., *Cut Loose Your Stammering Tongue: Black Theology in the Slave Narratives* (Maryknoll, N.Y.: Orbis Books), p. xxii.

63. *Ibid.*, p. xxi. Also see Dwight N. Hopkins, Shoes that Fit Our *Feet: Sources for a Constructive Black Theology* (Maryknoll, N.Y.: Orbis Books, 1993), pp. 1-218.

64. This contention courses through the thought of Sterling Stuckey and Lewis V. Baldwin, who insist that genuine freedom for African Americans requires an acceptance of how they have been shaped by African as well as Euro-American thought and traditions. See Stuckey, *Slave Culture*, pp. vii-97; and Baldwin, *"Invisible" Strands in African Methodism*, pp. 213-241.

Chapter Two

The Black Church and the Preacher During Slavery: Foundations of a Theology of Hope

The Church having opened the way for the development of the black man, other means have followed, and still others will follow until his opportunities are equal to that of any other race.... The African Church will then have accomplished its mission -- not till then.

J. W. Hoods

I soon saw a large field open in seeking and instructing my African brethren, who had been a long forgotten people and few of them attended public worship.

Richard Allen[2]

The assumption that African Americans had no theology during slavery is erroneous and must be challenged. While slaves and free Africans were not theologians in the eyes of their oppressors, or when judged by Western standards, they clearly expressed their creative ideas about the existence and nature of God and God's role in human affairs in their prayers, songs, sermons, and tales. Their theology was not shaped in the comfort of the Big House or the White House, but, rather, in the midst of a daily struggle against forces that sought to destroy their very humanity. Thus, theirs was an existential theology -- a theology rooted in their experience of suffering and in their conviction that God would ultimately free black people.[3]

African Americans in the antebellum period were sustained by a theology that stressed hope as essential to survival and for the achievement of freedom. This chapter holds that the sources of that theology of hope rested in the contributions of the black church and the black preacher toward the freedom of their people from slavery and racism. Because the church, under the leadership of the preacher, raised the God question in relation to the struggle against slavery and racism, the two greatest social evils of that time, it laid the foundations on which more contemporary black theologians could build.[4]

God Means Freedom: The Black Church Struggle Against Slavery and Racism

James H. Cone rightly argues that the organization of the first separate and independent black churches was "a visible manifestation of Black Theology."[15] This becomes all the more evident when one realizes that the black church was born in slavery and nurtured in the bosom of social protest. As early as the late eighteenth century, this institution spread its branches to the North and South, providing African Americans with an anti-slavery gospel and an institutional base and framework for an organized and sustained assault on the slave system.[6]

The independent African Church movement began as an organized effort in the late eighteenth century under the leadership of a Delaware ex-slave named Richard Allen. Convinced that slavery and racism contradicted the God revealed in the Bible, Allen led many Africans out of the predominantly white St. George's Methodist Episcopal Church in Philadelphia in 1787 and ultimately formed the African Methodist Episcopal Church.[7] Allen's example was followed by Peter Spencer, James Varick, George Liele, Andrew Bryan, and numerous other black leaders who saw the need for their people to take control of their own spiritual lives and destiny. The structures of white ecclesiastical dominance were abandoned, and black Methodist, Baptist, Presbyterian, and Episcopal Churches sprung up as a protest against white supremacy and as an affirmation of the need for black autonomy.[8]

Black preachers and laypersons insisted that the rise of independent black churches was consistent with the gospel and the entire Biblical revelation. In a sermon delivered in February, 1816, as the African Methodist Episcopal Church was developing, the A.M.E. preacher Daniel Coker compared his people's former situation in segregated white churches to that of the Jews in Babylon, and suggested that the God of the Israelites had made black ecclesiastical independence possible.[9] David Walker, the militant leader who enunciated the dominant themes of a black liberation theology in his celebrated Appeal (1829), praised Richard Allen for planting "a Church among us which will be as durable as the foundation of the earth on which it stands":

Richard Allen! Oh my God! The bare recollection of the labors of this man, and his ministers among his deplorably wretched brethren, (rendered so by the whites) to bring them to a knowledge of the God of Heaven, fills my soul with all those very high emotions which would take the pen of an Addison to portray. It is impossible my brethren for me to say much in this work respecting than man of God. When the Lord shall raise up coloured historians in succeeding generations, to present the crimes of this nation, to the then gazing world, the Holy Ghost will make them do justice to the name of Bishop Allen, of Philadelphia. Suffice it for me to say, that the name of this very man (Richard Allen) though now in obscurity and degradation, will notwithstanding, stand on the pages of history among the greatest divines who have lived since the apostolic age, and among the Africans, Bishop Allen's will be entirely preeminent.[10]

Two images of pre-Civil War black churches revealed their importance as symbols of hope and liberation among African Americans. One was that of "Old Israel," which suggested that the black church was called and commissioned to be a liberating, redemptive, and reconciling presence for blacks and whites alike.[11] Black churchpersons portrayed themselves as the Israel of old suffering under a new Pharaoh, and they discovered in the Exodus story a rich source of metaphors to explicate the unfolding history of themselves and the nation.[12] The belief was that God would free African slaves as He had liberated Israel. No where was this message of hope and liberation more prevalent than in the lyrics of the songs of the black church:

> When Israel was in Egypt's Land,
> Let my people go.
> Oppressed so hard they could not stand,
> Let my people go.
> Go down, Moses, way down in Egypt's Land,
> Tell old Pharaoh, let my people go.[13]

And there were these lines, which left no doubt about the slaves' conviction that their bondage was inconsistent with the divine plan for humanity:

> No more shall they in bondage toil,
> Let my people go.
> Let them come out with Egypt's spoil,
> Let my people go.[14]

The conviction coursing through the thought of black church persons was that God had chosen them for liberation at some designated time in the future. According to Lawrence W. Levine, "The most consistent single image the slave songs contain is that of the chosen people."[15] The fact that God had not yet acted in the history of African Americans as God had in the life of ancient Israel did not diminish the power of this image. Indeed, it became one of the cornerstones of antebellum black folk theology.

The second image of the antebellum black church was that of "all-comprehending institution," which, as stated previously, implied that the church was involved in every aspect of black life. Cut off from most areas of social and political life in the United States, African Americans found in the church not only an avenue for religious freedom and a force for fostering group cohesion and self-respect under difficult circumstances, but also opportunities for self-expression, recognition, and leadership.[16] Embodying the dual concerns of liberation in this world and salvation in the next, the church developed a wholistic approach to evangelism that involved both the preaching of the gospel and the performance of deeds in the interest of human liberation.

Black churches practically applied their theology of hope and liberation as they engaged in numerous movements to free their people. They boycotted slave-made goods, served as stations on the Underground Railroad, participated in militant phases of abolitionism, challenged segregation, and supported a convention movement designed to unite black churches across denominational boundaries to fight illiteracy, hunger, and poverty in African American communities.[17] Thus, an activist theology and spirituality found expression at a time when whites insisted on viewing black enslavement as an expression of the divine will, and on denouncing black churches as symbols of an unenlightened, superficial caricature of the Christian faith.

These developments cannot be understood apart from the shifts that were occurring in American theology generally in this period. The old rigid Calvinism was giving way to an Arminianized theology which inspired missionary and social outreach. Out of a growing revivalist spirit, fueled in part by the optimism surrounding the new nation and the move westward, there emerged Lyman Beecher, Charles G. Finney, and others who advanced and appropriated a perfectionist theology which encouraged the perfectibility of the individual as well as the improvement and/or rearrangement of the American social order. "Disinterested Benevolence," as elaborated by Samuel Hopkins and Nathaniel W. Taylor, was promoted as the key to Christian social responsibility, and local reform groups, service societies, and national organizations arose to take on the issues of colonization, slavery, women's rights, education, and missions. The black church did not escape the influence of these developments as it sought to promote both individual salvation and communal liberation.

William G. McLoughlin views this as a time when African Americans "had their own evangelical hope, which they furtively expressed in folktales and gospel songs."[20] As whites centered their optimism peculiarly on the new American nation, extolling its virtues and calling for the spread of its spiritual Christianity and democratic principles to the far corners of the earth, blacks criticized the nation's values and challenged it with a more prophetic and Bible-based vision of human freedom.[21] In their secret meetings characterized as the invisible institution, the slaves in the South, like black churchpersons in the North, nurtured a millennial hope that contrasted sharply with that of the whites:

> But the millennial goal of black Evangelicals was not the same as that of the white southern Evangelical; their Kingdom of God on earth did not include the continuation of slavery. Masking their desire for freedom behind a symbolic identification of slavery with that of the Jewish bondage in Egypt, black preachers and revivalists called metaphorically for a Moses to lead their people out of bondage. But their Canaan did not correspond with that of Northern Evangelicals, who hoped for total assimilation of

blacks, or of those who hoped that all blacks would find their Canaan in Africa. The black millennial dream of freedom and equality ran counter to the narrowing definition of what it meant to be an American that emerged from this awakening. Black Evangelical prophets saw more realistically than the white prophets of revitalization that a long hard road lay ahead.[22]

The idea of America's redemptive mission, driven largely by racism, was aimed by whites at the entire world. The idea was that the ultimate civilization of the dark world depended on the spread of America's spiritual and democratic values. This view permeated the theology of white Americans. In contrast, the black church's theology of hope and liberation embraced the needs of the African motherland as black Christians helped forge what Gayraud S. Wilmore calls "a connecting link between emigration, Christianity, and black nationalism."[23] Paul Cuffee, who founded the first African Baptist and Methodist Churches in Massachusetts and Rhode Island in the late eighteenth century, undertook missions to evangelize Africa and to "lay the foundation for forms of commerce between Africa and America that would compete with and finally bring an end to the slave trade."[24] Driven by similar concerns, Daniel Coker sailed for Africa with the assistance of the American Colonization Society, for it was his contention that colonization was "part of God's plan to bring the Christian faith to the land of his ancestors through the ministry of the black church."[25] While this whole ethos was rooted in an underestimation of the power and sophistication of African tribal religions and cultures, it was nevertheless consistent with the central thrust of nineteenth century black folk theology.

The high moral ground black Christians chose led many within the black church to assert a messianic role for them that extended beyond the limits of race and nationality. Having embraced a more inclusive Christian faith and theology than their oppressors, African Americans, declared David Walker in 1829, were ideally suited to evangelize the world:

> It is my solemn belief, that if ever the world becomes Christianized (which must certainly take place before long) it will be through the means, under God of the *Blacks*, who are now held in wretchedness, and degradation, by the white <u>Christians</u> of the world, who before they learn to do justice to us before our Maker ... send missionaries to convert the heathens, many of whom after they cease to worship gods, which neither see nor hear, become ten times more the children of Hell, then (sic) ever they were....[26]

The intense suffering of African Americans under slavery and racism reinforced the idea that they were better suited than whites to spread the Christian faith. This view was not surprising since blacks, in their spiritual songs, paralleled their suffering under slave masters to that of Jesus on the Cross. Sterling Brown claims that the slaves "fused belief and experiences in their portrayal of Calvary through song:

> Dey whupped him up de hill....
> Dey crowned his head with thorns...
> Dey pierced him in de side,
> An' de blood come a-twinklin' down;
> But he never said a mumbalin' word;
> Not a word; not a word.[27]

The image of the black church as a suffering community acting in the servant-style of Christ captured the imagination in striking ways, leading black leaders throughout the period of slavery to affirm David Walker's claims regarding its messianic potential. The black nationalist Martin Delany, with the mission of the black church deeply in mind, called upon his people to "do battle in the struggle now being made for the redemption of the world." "God himself as assuredly as he rules the destinies of nations," Delany added, "has presented these measures to us." But it was Delany's opinion that his people could never assume their messianic vocation as long as they lived among the whites, a position that under girded his call for the mass emigration of people of African descent from the United States to either Central America or some place in Africa.[28] Although Delany's views on emigrationism were never fully embraced as part of the liberation agenda of the black church, his perspective on the messianic potential of his people was clearly shared by Robert A. Young, Alexander Crummell, Edward W. Blyden, and other African American thinkers in antebellum America.

The black church's theology of hope was expressed in bolder terms as the Civil War began, particularly in the South where slavery was deeply entrenched. From the very beginning of the conflict, white and black churchpersons attached different religious meanings to it. Many Northern white Christians saw the war as part of a providential design for the redemption, unification, and salvation of the nation through the blood atonement of its most noble citizens.[29] Many Southern white Christians attributed the war to the wicked infidelity of the North and its rebellion against divine sovereignty.[30] For African Americans, the Civil War represented an enactment of Biblical principles which foretold the coming of the millennium. It was God's vehicle of deliverance -- a major step toward the realization of the black millennial dream of freedom and justice. It was evidence that the God who had delivered the Hebrews of old was still a liberating God. This theology of hope was profoundly expressed in black prayers, and biblical allusions filled the exclamations, sermons, songs, and reminiscences of the freedmen" once the Emancipation Proclamation took effect.[31] Lawrence W. Levine is correct in saying that slave songs became more openly anti-slavery and expressive of freedom, for African Americans sang, with renewed power, songs like "No More Auction Block," a Free at Last," "Before I'll Be a Slave," and "Child, Ain't You Glad You Got Out the Wilderness."[32]

The rejoicing that occurred in black churches after the Union Armies triumphed testified to the long-held conviction that slavery was not ultimately a part of God's plan for humanity. Indeed, the defeat of the rebel cause was an indication of how God becomes a co-worker and co-sufferer with God's creation in the building of greater human community.

The Moving Hand of God: The Black Preacher as Messenger of Hope

The relationship between preaching and the shaping of a theology of hope in the African American church tradition during slavery has not been sufficiently treated. Extant works which claim to explore the subject give only fleeting attention to the black church of the slave era, and their failure to make wide use of the slave narratives, sermons, and other sources from that period makes them all the more deficient.[33]

There was no greater symbol of hope and liberation among African Americans during slavery than the black preacher. Faced daily with physical and verbal abuse, African Americans found the strength to survive and the will to hope because of the presence and the words of the preacher. Preachers like Richard Allen, Peter Spencer, and James Varick fulfilled so many of the hopes and dreams of their people not only through the proclamation of a liberating gospel, but also through the organization of religious institutions that met their spiritual, ritualistic, and material needs. Allen, who became an African Methodist Episcopal bishop in 1816, consistently reminded his followers that God is "our deliverer," a word of assurance that struck a positive, responsive chord in the hearts of people who were told daily that they were less than human.[34] He, Spencer, and Varick were abolitionist preachers who proclaimed that God would not long tolerate injustice.

Allen was among the first of a long line of black preachers who made Psalms 68:31 one of the cornerstones of their theology of hope and liberation. That passage reads: "Princess shall come out of Egypt; Ethiopia shall soon stretch out her hands unto God." Here the black preacher found ample proof that the children of Africa would one day find their rightful place among the great mass of free humanity in every part of the globe. This great prophesy, which echoed through the sermons of black preachers in the ante-bellum North, became a forecast of the ultimate fulfillment of the people's spiritual yearning."[35]

The extent to which slave preachers in the South preached from this text is not known. It is known that the sermons of slave preachers were saturated with Biblical phrases, images, and symbols, but they were also clothed in simple language and aimed at the day-to-day problems that the enslaved encountered in the fields and at the Big House. With the lash, the auction block, and the shackles so visibly present in the slave experience, the slaves found in the preacher and his words the strength to face life with an indomitable faith:

> The antebellum Negro preacher was the greatest single factor in determining the spiritual destiny of the slave community. He it was who gave to the masses of his fellows a point of view that became for them a veritable Door of Hope. His ministry was greatly restricted as to movement, function, and opportunities of leadership, but he was blessed with one important insight: he was convinced that every human being was a child of God. This belief included the slave as well as the master. When he

spoke to his group on an occasional Sabbath day, he knew what they had lived through during the weeks; how their total environment had conspired to din into their minds and spirits the corroding notion that as human beings they were of no significance. Thus his one message springing full grown from the mind of God repeated in many ways a wide range of variations; "You are created in God's image. You are not slaves, you are not niggers; you are God's children." Many weary, spiritually and physically exhausted slaves found new strength and power gushing up into all the reaches of their personalities, inspired by the words that fell from this man's lips. He had discovered that which religion insists is the ultimate truth about human life and destiny. It is the supreme validation of the human spirit. He who knows this is able to transcend the vicissitudes of life, however terrifying, and look out on the world with quiet eyes.[36]

These reflections, penned by the black theologian and mystic Howard Thurman, are consistent with James Weldon Johnson's characterization of the preacher as "a mainspring of hope and inspiration."[37] The reflections of both Thurman and Johnson are borne out in slave testimony. Louis Hughes, born a slave in Virginia in 1832, explained how the slave preacher lifted his people up into a transcendent moment, thus preparing them to deal psychologically with yet another day in bondage:

The words that came from the minister were always of a consolatory kind. He knew the crosses of his fellow slaves and their hardships, for he had shared them himself.... After singing he would always speak to them of the necessity for patience in bearing the crosses, urging them to endure as good soldiers. Many tears were shed, and many glad shouts of praise would burst forth during the sermon.[38]

It was the caring function of the preacher's ministry on the plantation that led W. E. B. DuBois to refer to him as a <u>priest</u>. The image of priest cast the preacher in the role of ritual leader, for he, as mentioned previously, became a mediator between God and the people, and between the living and the dead, in order to ease the pain of living. He demonstrated the divine presence and will among his people, and allowed them to participate with him in a special relationship with God. Dubois has provided the best description of the full range of the slave preacher's contributions as priest:

> He early appeared on the plantation and found his function as the healer of the sick, the interpreter of the Unknown, the comforter of the sorrowing, the supernatural avenger of wrong, and the one who rudely picturesquely expressed the longing, disappointment, and resentment of a stolen and oppressed people.[39]

Thus, the preacher helped his people to experience a sense of freedom and wholeness that transcended their physical bondage. The effect was essentially the liberation of the human spirit and the freedom to define ones self despite that wall of assumptions that white oppressors sought to impose on black humanity.

But the sermons of the preacher spoke to the need for physical liberation as well. As slaves listened to the sermons of their preachers on the story of the Exodus, they were assured that the God who guided the Israelites from Egypt through the wilderness into Canaan land would one day free their bodies from the chains that confined them. The ex-slave Simon Brown of Virginia recalled the joy, relief, and feelings of eager expecta-

tion that came when slaves heard the account of God's dealings
with Israel:

> When the Bible told how Moses made old King
> Pharaoh turn all the Hebrew slaves loose away down in
> Egypt land, we black "raves thought we must be like
> those Jews in God's sight. And one day God would send
> a mighty man into our slave land and set us all free. Now
> that kind of God I can love and serve. But the white
> preacher in his sermons never did say a word about God
> setting the black man free. No, sir, not a word."[40]

The message of black preachers in the South and North was
that God's word in the scriptures affirmed the liberation of all
persons, a view that stood in stark contrast to the tendency of
white preachers to sanction and justify human oppression with
references to Ephesians 6:5, the Epistle to Philemon, and other
parts of the Bibles.[41] Ex-slave Sarah Ford of Texas remembered
that the preacher on her plantation was sent to the cotton field
as punishment for his insistence that whites were not naturally
superior to blacks:

> One day Uncle Lew preachin' and he say "De Lawd
> make everyone to come in unity on de level, both white
> and black!" When Massa Charles hears 'bout it, he don't
> like it none, and de next mornin' old Uncle Jake git Uncle
> Lew and put him in de field with de rest.[42]

Clearly, the slave preachers knew the difference between
Bible Christianity and Christianity as defined and taught by
their enslavers. But the restrictions imposed by the slave system often made it impossible for them to publicly express the
difference among their fellow slaves, especially when whites

were among their listeners. To deal with such restrictions, many slave preachers gave one message to their people in the presence of whites and quite another when whites were absent, thus calling to mind the cleverness of Brer Rabbit as revealed in slave tales. The account of ex-slave Anderson Edwards of Texas illustrates the point:

> When I starts preachin', I couldn't read or write and had to preach what masse told me. He say tell them niggers iffen they obeys the master they goes to Heaven; but I knowed there's something better for them, but daren't tell them 'cept on the sly. That I done lots. I tell 'em iffen they keep praying, the Lord will set 'em free.[43]

Ex-slave Litt Young, born a slave in Mississippi in 1850, recalled a preacher who was equally clever:

> ...a yellow man preached to us. She (mistress) had him preach how we was to obey our master and missy if we want to go to Heaven, but when she wasn't there, he come out with straight preachin' from the Bible.[44]

The preachers in the slave quarters knew that the message of hope and freedom they had to share with fellow bondspersons was dangerous and could lead to severe penalties, even death. The ex-slave Simon Brown, who as a boy often alerted slaves when whites approached their secret religious meetings, reported the following concerning the ingenuity shown by a slave preacher under difficult circumstances:

> While I watched down the road, I listed to what went on inside. The preacher was praying to the Lord something like this: "Oh, Lord, look down in pity on us poor

slaves. Please, Lord, the load of slavery is so heavy it's about to destroy us all. The grass in the cotton field is so high. The sun is so hot. We almost perish in the middle of the day. Do, Master, have mercy and help us please." And the folks inside shouted, "Yes, Lord," and "Amen," and carried on.... Then I heard the pater-rollers on their horses cantering up the road, coming to the meeting house. Quickly I cracked the door and hollered inside, "Pater-rollers are coming! Pater-rollers are coming!" And when those white men rode up in the yard, they listened to what the slave preacher was saying. By then the preacher had changed his prayer and was saying, "Please, Jesus, help us poor creatures to be faithful to old Master and old Missy. Enable us to do the task in the field tomorrow that they set for us. Help us to be faithful servants and obey our masters. Please, Sir, hear our prayer." ....When those pater-rollers heard that, they said, "Everything's all right in there," and they jumped on their horses and galloped away down the road. Then I cracked the door again and yelled, "The pater-rollers are gone. The pater-rollers are gone." The preacher man smiled and lifted his arms and said, "Do, Jesus, forgive us for those lies we just prayed, for you know how hard we suffer down here and how we pray for freedom. And then all the people went back to singing and praying for deliverance from their troubles.[45]

The judgment and punishment that awaited slave owners permeated the sermons of black preachers, North and South, and these themes were very much a part of the folk theology of hope and liberation. Richard Allen's and Peter Spencer's assertion that God's wrath would be visited upon the heads of slave owners squared with Brother Coteny's insistence that the goats would be separated from the sheep at the judgment. The belief that the goats would be doomed to eternal punishment and the sheep to everlasting life ran through the sermons of this slave preacher, a message quite revealing since whites were goats and blacks were sheep in slave folklore. Brother Coteny's reflections on what would ultimately be the fate of white enslavers testifies to the slave preacher's ability to use cryptic or hidden language to reveal dangerous thoughts, a quality also evident in the spirituals.[46]

The slaves themselves did not escape the indictment of their preachers, for they, too, were held to high standards of Christian accountability. The situation could not have been otherwise since the slave preacher typically made no distinction between the need for liberation in this world and salvation in the next. Thus, a part of the preacher's liberating gospel involved admonishing the slaves to live as far above sin as possible. The ex-slave Simon Brown recounted that

The slave preacher or leader would call for the sinners to come forward and sit on the mourner's bench, right in front of him where he could preach straight at them. He would call out each one's sins to his or her face. Now, if a man was a gambler, the preacher'd say, "Gambler, you better get ready; you got to die." And when he got through picturing the poor sinners a-suffering in the fires of everlasting torment, he'd command them all to "fall on your knees at the mourner's bench and pray to be saved before you die."[47]

The widespread view that the preacher's proclamations about heaven had little or nothing to do with freedom in this life is not persuasive, especially given the interrelationship between this worldly and other-worldly concerns in slave art. The other-worldliness coursing through the slave sermons, as Gayraud S. Wilmore points out, was essentially non interim strategy":

> The "otherworldliness" of slave preaching was nothing less than an interim strategy. It was the deliberate choice of the preacher to give his people something to which they could attach their tumultuous emotions -- something to substitute for the immediate, uncontrollable and probably ill-fated decision to experience, then and there, the freedom which Christ had promised. He gave, thereby, relief from the tragedy of life in slavery, a modicum of comfort in the presence of the overwhelming reality of defeat and despair."[48]

Interestingly enough, the visions of freedom and hope were most evident when the slave preacher focused on the joys of heaven. A perfect illustration of this occurred when the slave preacher said his final words over Sister Dicey, the faithful old slave woman in Virginia. While celebrating Sister Dicey's journey into the afterlife where unfettered freedom awaited her, the words of the preacher actually promoted the struggle for communal freedom among her survivors, thus recalling Brer rabbit's role among the little creatures in an atmosphere frequented by big, dangerous, and more powerful animals:

> ...the slave preacher said words of comfort over the body -- something like this: "Sister Dicey, since God in His mercy has taken your soul from earth to Heaven and out of your misery, I commit your body to the ground, earth to earth, ashes to ashes, dust to dust, where it will rest in peace. But on that Great, Getting Up Morning, when the trumpet of God shall sound to wake up all the dead, we will meet you in the skies and join the hosts of

saints who will go marching in. Yes, we want to be in that number, Sister Dicey, when the saints go marching in. ...Before the preacher could finish his Benediction, some of the women got so happy that they drowned him out with their singing and handclapping and shouting.[49]

The gospel of liberation and hope stands as a vital part of the rich legacy passed down by the antebellum black church and the black preacher. That legacy reminds one of the power and genius of the African American religious heritage and of the pivotal importance of the preacher in the shaping of black protest thought.

Contemporary Black Theologians and SlaveThought: Building on a Tradition

The relationship between hope and freedom for the oppressed has been carefully treated in the writings of Major J. Jones. Jones contends that no Christian theology of hope can overlook the promises of God through Jesus Christ for those who suffer from the forces of oppression. Moreover, he suggests that the only hope black theology has in the future is to become a theology of hope. But Jones grounds his understanding of hope in the theological reflections of the German theologian Jurgen Moltmann, failing to sufficiently show how that theme is the basis of black theologians' cultural bond with blacks of the slavery era, and particularly with the black church and the black preacher.[51]

The Exodus story as articulated by the black church and the preacher during slavery remains the richest paradigm for the explication of a black theology of hope for today and tomorrow. Martin Luther King, Jr. recognized this in the 1950s and 1960s, and he drew on the traditions of the antebellum black church and the slave preacher in articulating his vision of hope and community. King clearly found in these traditions a theology of hope. Thus, he drew on the insights of slave songs and the wisdom of the slave preacher in explaining how his people were moving through the Egypt of slavery, the wilderness of segregation, and on into the promised land of freedom, justice, and equality of opportunity.[52]

William R. Jones's contention that the Exodus event is not applicable to the black struggle can render the black theistic tradition useless for the shaping of a black theology of hope for the future if it is taken seriously.[53] The Exodus story belongs as much to the black church tradition as to any other tradition, and it holds the key to any future theology of hope that speaks to racism, sexism, classism that haunts the African American community.

A group of young black theologians are emerging who are taking slave thought and sources seriously for doing contemporary black theology. They are George C. L. Cummings, Will Coleman, and Dwight N. Hopkins. Cummings concludes that slave ideas concerning the Christian spirit and the coming of God's Kingdom were grounded in perspectives that "convey the fundamental hopes of black oppressed people."[54] Coleman treats slave stories in terms of their language of liberation, a theme that stands at the core of black theology today. Hopkins concludes that the slaves fashioned a Christian theology out of a combination of African religious values and elements of the Christian faith.[55] In a more extensive work, Hopkins deals with slave narratives, stories, and other folk traditions as resources for understanding slave theology, and for constructing a viable theology today. All of these scholars correctly assume that the slaves were liberationists, a view that has been questioned by other young black theologians such as Victor Anderson.[56]

The failure of most black theologians to take seriously slave traditions as a foundation for doing theology is obviously connected with their intense desire to find full acceptance for themselves and their writings in the academy. Since the rise of black theology, most of its shapers have operated within the context of white academic establishments where respect for slave traditions is virtually non-existent. This explains why black theologians have, since the 1960s, drawn more heavily on white Western theologians than on slave thought for insights and for the legitimation of their own ideas. The suggestion that slave testimony, as revealed in tales, narratives, songs, and a variety of other sources, is less legitimate and useful than the thoughts and models of white Western theological traditions accounts in part for the failure of black theologians in the academy to communicate with most clergy and laity in the black church.[57]

The need for a reconstruction of black theology based on a wider respect for and use of the traditions of the black preacher and the black church during slavery cannot be logically denied. It is the conviction of this author that black theology will not assume its true identity and authenticity, apart from Euro-American traditions, until it takes seriously the messages of hope and liberation that echoes through the sermons of slave preachers and the ethos and style of the antebellum black church.

Endnotes

1. Quoted in Gayraud S. Wilmore, *Black Religion and Black Radicalism: An Interpretation of the Religious History of Afro-American People* (Maryknoll, N. Y.: Orbis Books, 1983), p. 74

2. Richard Allen, *The Life, Experience and Gospel Labors of the Rt. Rev. Richard Allen* (Nashville: The A.M.E. Sunday School Union, n.d.; originally published in 1833), p. 14.

3. This point is developed at some length in James H. Cone, *Black Theology and Black Power* (New York: The Seabury Press, 1969), pp. 116-123; and James H. Cone, *A Black Theology of Liberation* (Philadelphia: J. B. Lippincott Company, 1970), pp. 22-249.

4. Strangely enough, James H. Cone does not include the theological traditions of the slaves among the contexts for the origin of contemporary black theology. Describing those contexts as the civil rights movement of the 1950s and 1960s, the publication of Joseph Washington's *Black Religion* (1964), and the rise of black power, Cone leaves the erroneous impression that what blacks in the antebellum period thought about God in relation to their struggle had no direct bearing on the development of contemporary black theology as an intellectual discipline. See James H. Cone, *For My People -- Black Theology and the Black Church: Where Have We Been and Where are We Going?* (Maryknoll, N. Y.: Orbis Books, 1984), pp. 6-30. One source which skillfully links the theological traditions of the slaves to more contemporary developments in black liberation theology is Lewis V. Baldwin, *To Make the Wounded Whole: The Cultural Legacy of Martin Luther King, Jr.* (Minneapolis:Fortress Press, 1992), pp. 63-69.

5. Cone, *A Black Theology of Liberation*, p. 59.

6. This perspective is developed in Wilmore, *Black Religion and Black Radicalism*, pp. 74-98.

7. The events leading up to the founding of the African Methodist Episcopal Church are recorded in Allen, *The Life, Experience and Gospel Labors*, pp. 7-31.

8. The origins of the separate and independent black church movement is treated in a number of works. See Carter G. Woodson, *The History of the Negro Church* (Washington, D.C.: The Associated Publishers, 1921), pp. 61-129; Carol V. R. George, *Segregated Sabbaths: Richard Allen and*

The Black Church and the Preacher During Slavery: Foundations of a Theology of Hope

the Rise of Independent Black Churches, 1760-1840 (New York: Oxford University Press, 1973), pp. 3-183; Wilmore, *Black Religion and Black Radicalism*, pp. 74-98; and Lewis V. Baldwin, *"Invisible" Strands in African Methodism: A History of the African Union Methodist Protestant and Union American Methodist Episcopal Churches, 1805-1980* (Metuchen, N. J.: Scarecrow Press, 1983), pp. 37-147.

9. Daniel Coker, *Sermon Delivered Extempore in the African Methodist Episcopal Church in the City of Baltimore. on the 21st of January. 1816. to a Numerous Concourse of People, on Account of the Colored People Gaining Their Church (Bethel) in the Supreme Court of the State of Pennsylvania*, in Herbert Aptheker, ed., *A Documentary History of the Negro People in the United States*, I (New York: Citadel Press, 1951), pp. 67-69; and George, *Segregated Sabbaths*, pp. 85-86.

10. Charles M. Wiltse, ed., *David Walker's Appeal' in Four Articles: Together with a Preamble to the Coloured Citizens of the World* (New York: Hill and Wang, 1965; originally published in 1829), pp. 58-59.

11. This image of the antebellum black church is explored in Albert J. Raboteau, *A Fire in the Bones: Reflections on African-American Religious History* (Boston: Beacon Press, 1995), pp. 17-36; and Peter Hodgson, *Revisioning the Church: Ecclesial Life Under a New Paradigm* (Philadelphia: Fortress Press, 1989),

12. Paul E. Johnson, ed., *African-American Christianity: Essays in History* (Berkeley: University of California Press, 1994), pp. 9-15; and Baldwin, *Intake the Wounded Whole*, pp. 81-82.

13. Quoted in Harold Courlander, *Negro Folk Music, U.S.A.* (New York: Columbia University Press, 1963), p. 42.

14. *Ibid.*

15. Lawrence W. Levine, *Black Culture and Black Consciousness: Afro-American Folk Thought from Slavery to Freedom* (New York: Oxford University Press, 1977), pp. 33-34.

16. Winthrop S. Hudson, *Religion in America: An Historical Account of the Development of American Religious Life* (New York: Charles Scribner's Sons, 1965), pp. 22S and 351.

17. Frederick A. Norwood, *The Story of American Methodism: A History of the United Methodists and Their Relations* (Nashville: Abingdon Press, 1974), p. 171; Alain Rogers, *"The African Methodist Episcopal Church, A Study in Black Nationalism," The Black Church*, I

(1972), pp. 17-43; Baldwin, *"Invisibles Strands in African Methodism,*
pp. 61-69 and 143146; and Wilmore, *Black Religion and Black Radicalism*, pp. 101-109.

18. Hudson, *Religion in America*, pp. 152-153.

19. Few scholars have sought to understand the functions of the antebellum black church in this wider context. An exception is Lewis V. Baldwin, *The Mark of a Man: Peter Spencer and the African Union Methodist Tradition* (Lanham, Md.: University Press of America, 1987), p. 33.

20. William G. McLoughlin, *Revivals, Awakenings, and Reform: An Essay on Religion and Social Chance in America*, 1607-1977 (Chicago: The University of Chicago Press, 1978), p. 138.

21. See Ernest Lee Tuveson, *Redeemer Nation: The Idea of America's Millennial Role* (Chicago: the University of Chicago Press, 1968), pp. 1-214; and McLoughlin, *Revivals, Awakenings, and Reform*, p. 138.

22. McLoughlin, *Revivals, Awakenings. and Reform*, p. 138.

23. Wilmore, *Black Religion and Black Radicalism*, p. 101.

24. *Ibid.*, p. 100; and John H. Bracey, Jr., et. al., eds., *Black Nationalism in America* (Indianapolis: Bobbs-Merrill, 1970), p. xxxi.

25. Wilmore, *Black Religion and Black Radicalism*, p. 104.

26. Wiltse, ed., *David Walker's Appeal*, p. 18; and Sterling Stuckey, *Slave Culture: Nationalist Theory and the Foundations of Black America* (New York: Oxford University Press, 1987), p. 132.

27. Sterling Brown, "Negro Folk Expression: Spirituals, Seculars, Ballads and Work Songs," in August Meter and Elliot Rudwick, eds., *The Making of Black America: The Black Community in Modern America*, 2 Vols. (New York: Atheneum, 1974), II, pp. 212-213; and Lewis V. Baldwin, *"'Deliverance to the Captives': Images of Jesus Christ in the Minds of Afro-American Slaves," Journal of Religious Studies*, 12, no. 2, pp. 32-33.

28. Wilmore, *Religion and Black Radicalism*, pp. 111-112; Sterling Stuckey, ed., *The Ideological Origins of Black Rationalism* (Boston: Beacon Press, 1972), pp. 21-29 and 195236.

29. This was certainly the view espoused in Horace Bushnell's Tour Obligations to the Dead (1865), included in William G. McLaughlin,

ed., *The American Evangelicals, 1800-1900: An Anthology* (Gloucester, Mass.: Peter Smith, 1976), pp. 141-157.

30. See Gardiner H. Shattuck, Jr., *A Shield and Hiding Place: The Religious Life of the Civil War Armies* (Macon, Ga.: Mercer University Press, 1987), pp. 1-12.

31. Levine, *Black Culture and Black Consciousness*, pp. 136-138.

32. *Ibid.*

33. Examples are James H. Harris, *Pastoral Theology: A Black Church Perspective* (Minneapolis: Fortress Press, 1991), pp. 3-129; and Olin P. Moyd, *The Sacred Art: Preaching and Theology in the African American Tradition* (Valley Forge, Pa.: Judson Press, 1995), pp. 1-138. Harris does examine the subject in one of his most recent works, but he fails to draw sufficiently on slave sources. See James H. Harris, *Preaching Liberation* (Minneapolis: Fortress Press, 1995), pp. 38-50.

34. Allen, *The Life, Experience and Gospel Labors*, pp. 17-18.

35. Wilmore, *Black Religion and Black Radicalism*, p. 121.

36. Howard Thurman, *Deep River: Reflections on the Religious Insights of Certain of the Negro Spirituals* (Richmond, Ind.: Friends United Press, 1975), pp. 17-18.

37. James Weldon Johnson, *God's Trombones: Seven Negro Sermons in Verse* (New York: Viking Press, 1927), pp. 2-3.

38. Louis Hughes, *Thirty Years a Slave* (New York: Negro Universities Press, 1969; originally published in 1897), pp. 52-54.

39. John Hope Franklin, ed., *The Souls of Black Folk in Three Negro Classics* (New York: Avon Books, 1965), p. 342.

40. William J. Faulkner, *The Days When the Animals Talked: Black American Folktales and How They Came to Be* (Chicago: Follett Publishing Company, 1977), p. 53.

41. Wilmore, *Black Religion and Black Radicalism*, p. 9.

42. George P. Rawick, ed., *The American Slave, A Composite Autobiography: Texas Narratives* (Westport, Conn.: Greenwood Press, 1977), XVI, part 2, p. 44.

43. Quoted in Levine, *Black Culture and Black Consciousness*, pp. 48 and 81-135.

44. Rawick, ed., *Texas Narratives*, XVI, part 2, p. 228.

45. Faulkner, *The Days When the Animals Talked*, pp. 30-31.

46. Rev. John G. Williams, *"De Ole Plantation"* (Charleston, S. C.: Walter Evans & Cogswell Company, 1895), pp. 8-11; and Eugene D. Genovese, *Roll, Jordan, Roll: The World the Slaves Made* (New York: Pantheon Books, 1972), pp. 265-266.

47. Faulkner, *The Days When the Animals Talked*, pp. 54-55.

48. Wilmore, *Black Religion and Black Radicalism*, p. 51.

49. Faulkner, *The Days When the Animals Talked*, pp. 38-39.

50. Major J. Jones, *Black Awareness: A Theology of Hope* (Nashville: Abingdon Press, 1971), pp. 11-17.

51. This point is advanced in Lewis V. Baldwin, *To Make the Wounded Whole: The Cultural Legacy of Martin Luther King. Jr.* (Minneapolis: Fortress Press, 1992), p. 106.

52. *Ibid.*, pp. 64-64.

53. William R. Jones, *Is God a White Racist: A Preamble to Black Theology* (NEW York: Doubleday & Company, 1973), pp. 18162.

54. Dwight N. Hopkins and George C. L. Cummings, eds., *Cut Loose Your Stammering Tongue: Black Theology in the Slave Narratives* (Maryknoll, N.Y.: Orbis Books, 1991), pp. xxii and 46-66.

55. *Ibid.*, pp. xxi-xxii, 1-45, and 67-102.

56. Dwight N. Hopkins, *Shoes that Fit Our Feet: Sources for a Constructive Black Theology* (Maryknoll, N.Y.: Orbis Books, 1993), pp. 1-218.

57. This concern is raised and addressed to some extent, though not thoroughly, in James H. Harris, *Pastoral Theology: A Black Church Perspective* (Minneapolis: Fortress Press, 1991), pp. 3-129.

Chapter Three

From Reconstruction to the Age of Jim Crow: The Black Preacher, the Church, and the God Question

O God? How long shall the mounting flood of innocent blood roar in-shine ears and pound in our hearts for vengeance? Forgive us, good Lord, we know not what we say! Bewildered we are and passion-tossed, mad with the madness of a mobbed and mocked and murdered people; straining at the armposts of Thy throne, we raise our shackled hands and charge Thee, God, by the bones of our stolen fathers, by the tears of our dead mothers, by the very blood of Thy crucified Christ: What meaneth this? Tell us the plan; give us the sign!

W. E. B. DuBois[1]

...we solemnly raise our voice against the horrible crimes of lynch law as practiced in the South, and we call upon Christians everywhere to do the same or be branded as sympathizers with the murderers.

Ida B. Wells[2]

The signing of the Emancipation Proclamation by President Abraham Lincoln in 1863 and the climax of the Civil War two years later confronted both the black preacher and the black church with many social, economic, and political challenges. Homeless, illiterate, and devoid of economic resources, some four million black men, women, and children, freed from the old plantation system, were forced to confront a white world that became increasingly hostile and determined to maintain the structures of white supremacy.[3] In what appeared to be a new found freedom, black preachers were compelled to make the gospel and the entire Biblical revelation relevant to the changing situation of their people. Black churches, still the only institution owned by African Americans on a wide scale, were compelled to devise and implement ministry and mission on an unprecedented scale.[4]

The sheer gravity of the situation demanded not only strategies and programs for the social, economic, and political advancement of African Americans, but also a vision of God that could sustain them spiritually and psychologically. The various responses of black preachers and churches to the black condition in the period from 1865 to 1955, and the significance of their thought and activities for black theology, are the focus of this chapter. The attention devoted to this period is particularly important in view of the contention that the black folk theology of hope and liberation, which had emerged out of the slave experience, surrendered to the image of the patient, long-suffering, white God who appeared to bless the status quo.[5]

Reconstruction and Beyond: Linking Theology and Programs of Uplift

For the black clergy and laity who addressed the enormous problems of black freedom and survival during Reconstruction, theology had to move beyond the theoretical to engage the practical. This inescapable need was occasioned by the adoption of the Thirteenth Amendment in 1865, the Civil Rights Bill in 1866, the Fourteenth Amendment in 1868, and the Fifteenth Amendment in 1870, pieces of legislation that recognized black citizenship and legitimated the access of African Americans in the South to the ballot and to public office for the very first time.[6] Black preachers and churches responded with philosophies and programs of uplift that were consistent with their understandings of scripture and of the activity of God in history.

Black preachers sought to reinforce in the minds of their people the kind of folk theology that had pervaded much of church life in antebellum times. The central convictions were that slavery had been destroyed as an act of God's punishment of America, that the God of the Bible was not oblivious to black life, and that this God demanded the full participation of African Americans in the daily functions of society. This message echoed through the sermon that Henry Highland Garnet, the black Presbyterian minister and nationalist, delivered before the United States Congress on February 12, 1865.[7] In an emotional moment, Garnet called upon both blacks and whites to leave the harsh realities of slavery behind them and, with God's help, to work collectively toward the realization of a just and inclusive society:

> The nation has begun its exodus from worst than Egyptian bondage; and I beseech you that you say to the people that they go forward. With the assurance of God's favor in all things done in obedience to his righteous will, and guided by day and by night by the pillars of cloud and fire, let us not pause until we have reached the other and safe side of the stormy and crimson sea. Let free men and patriots mete out complete and equal justice to all men and thus prove to mankind the superiority of our democratic, republican government.[8]

Preachers and churches in the African American community took the lead in demonstrating the power and superiority of the American democratic system. Black churches, under the leadership of preachers, contributed in this regard through an enhancement of their historic role as "all-comprehending institutions."[9] They sought to bring stability to black families that had been seriously fragmented during slavery. Family members who had been sold from plantation to plantation via the domestic slave trade were in some cases located with their assistance, and some families were reunited. To bring greater strength to the family structure, black churches encouraged the sanctity of the marriage vow, punished unconventional sex behavior, and insisted on the necessity for fathers to be strong heads of and providers for their families.[10] The pervasive belief among black preachers and their congregations was that strong families and solid family values contribute to the type of organized social life that is the bedrock of any democratic society.

Some of the most remarkable contributions of black churches occurred in the economic sphere. Convinced that in this democracy African Americans should have their share of the economy where separate people function beside each other, exchanging the power they control for that held by other races or ethnic groups, black churches and their leaders urged their people to be industrious and frugal, to pool their resources, to purchase land and buildings, to be prompt in paying debts, and to support one another in business enterprises. Benevolent and mutual aid societies, which had existed in black churches in the North in antebellum times, were organized and reorganized to meet the material needs of the widowed, the sick and handicapped, the orphaned, and the imprisoned. The names of many of theses societies were taken from the Bible, such as "The Builders of the Walls of Jericho" and "The Sons and Daughters of Esther. In their function as vehicles of economic cooperation, black churches had an even greater claim to what has been termed a theology of uplifted.[12]

Perhaps the greatest challenge before black churches and preachers in the three decades after the Civil War rested in the area of education. Denied even the most basic education in slavery times, thousands of African Americans in the South cried out for the opportunity to read and write. Churches established elementary and secondary schools, Bible institutes and seminaries, and colleges. By 1900, black Baptist churches were underwriting about ninety secondary schools and colleges, the African Methodist Episcopal Church (A.M.E.) was sustaining thirty-two, the African Methodist Episcopal Zion Church (A.M.E.Z.) claimed eight, and the Christian Methodist Episcopal Church five.[13] These institutions provided basic as well as Biblical and moral education, with the aim of preparing African Americans to live productive lives and to participate fully in the American democratic processes. For many black preachers, Jesus' admonition to love God "with all your mind" (Mark 12:30 RSV) afforded the greatest challenge for the church in the field of education.

Education was all the more important since African Americans in the South had the right to vote and hold political offices. Black churches combined their role as educational centers with their contributions as arenas of political life. Churches instructed the folk in the wise use of the ballot, and became the proving ground for black political leadership. Black preachers, who were more apt than lay persons to have some form of education, held various political offices. Henry M. Turner, the A.M.E. Preacher, served as a legislator and postmaster in Georgia, and as a Republican organizer for that state and South Carolina. Hiram R. Revels, another A.M.E. minister, was elected the first black senator in Mississippi in 1870.[14] Numerous other black preachers assumed political offices throughout the South, suggesting the tendency of African Americans not to separate the sacred from the secular, or the religious from the political. Moreover, this was a clear indication of how the folk theology of hope and liberation nurtured in the church found practical application. Indeed, theology and praxis came together in unique and unprecedented ways.

This became all the more evident since black churches refused to separate their efforts for social and political advancement from their determination to win the world for Christ. In fact, a sense of missionary urgency and compassion pervaded the ethos of the church, as it sought to implement the mandate of Jesus Christ as set forth in the Great Commission (Matthew 28:19-20 RSV). Baptists, Methodists, Presbyterians, and blacks from other denominations left the North and moved South to evangelize ex-slaves who had previously worshipped in predominantly white churches, or who had been a part of the secret meetings called the "invisible institution."[15] These churches also got involved in foreign missions, efforts which increased their memberships significantly. "In undertaking this endeavor," writes Clarence E. Walker, "A.M.E. missionaries believed that they were instruments of God's will, that God had given their church a special task -- to uplift the black race in America and then in the world."[16]

As black preachers and churches related their God concepts to sustained efforts to elevate the race socially, economically, intellectually, politically, and spiritually, they encountered strong resistance from white terrorists and mobs. The Ku Klux Klan was organized in 1866 in Pulaski, Tennessee, and, for the next thirty years, it was a major part of white racist efforts to beat back the tide of black advancement.[17] Hundreds of African Americans were beaten, maimed, and killed, and black voters and public officials were physically and verbally attacked as well. The social and political rights of African Americans slowly eroded, and, as John Hope Franklin notes, "By 1898 the pattern for the constitutional disfranchisement of the Negro had been completely drawn."[18] The revitalized theology of hope that had developed with the abolishment of slavery and the recognition of black citizenship rights in the South, gave way to feelings of frustration and questions about the meaning of the black experience and God's role in it. It was in this context that the black church became what E. Franklin Frazier calls "a refuge in a hostile white world," providing for African Americans "a means of catharsis for their pent-up emotions and frustrations."[19]

While traditional black church teachings emphasized concern for the poor and oppressed, not all African American churchpersons were in agreement as to how this concern should be manifested. When it came to this issue, there were four general categories of black clergy, who normally set the pattern for what black lay-persons generally believed: the pietistic perfectionists, who avoided social and political involvements while proclaiming the word of God and focusing their people's attention on the glories of heaven; progressive accommodationist clergy, who felt that religion should assist blacks in adjusting to their condition and the status quo; prophetic pragmatists, who believed that spiritual values should be a central force in transforming the society and culture; and religious nationalists, who employed religious concepts and themes in justifying the need for African Americans to separate completely from the white racist society.[20]

Representative of the pietistic perfectionists was Daniel J. Russell, a leading minister in the A.M.E. Zion Church before rejoining the African Union First Colored Methodist Protestant Church (A.U.F.C.M.P.), based in Wilmington, Delaware. Born in Delaware in 1846, Russell also embodied characteristics of progressive accommodationism, but his primary identification rested with the pietistic perfectionists.[21] Russell stressed the need in his sermons and writings for the perfectibility of the individual, giving special attention to the necessity of being filled with the Holy Ghost and preparing for salvation in the next world. Refusing to challenge white power and the status quo, he apparently assumed that personal conversion and devotion were the only avenues to the perfectibility of society.[22] In taking such an approach, Russell spoke for many constituents of both the A.M.E. Zion and the A.U.F. C.M.P. Churches.

75

Progressive accommodationism seems to have found a proponent in Bishop Jacob F. Ramsey of the Union American Methodist Episcopal Church (U.A.M.E.). Born in New Jersey in 1851, Ramsey, like Russell, did not get involved in the agitation for black rights in the late nineteenth century. He believed that the advancement of African Americans could occur best and easier through exemplary conduct on their part, and also through learning from European-American church traditions and cooperating with the status quo.[23] This conviction and approach, which found classic expression in Booker T. Washington's "Atlanta Exposition Address" (1894), secured the allegiance of many black clergy and laypersons in the black church.[24] However, Progressive accommodationism, like pietistic perfectionism, ran counter to the folk theology of liberation that had led decades earlier to separate and independent black churches.

Prophetic pragmatism was exemplified in the late nineteenth century by William E. Walker, a black Baptist preacher from Virginia. Walker, like numerous black clergypersons before him, stood squarely in the tradition of ancient Hebrew Prophets like Amos, who denounced the mistreatment of the poor and humble by the privileged. Declaring in 1873 that "Man is not free after leaving the land of Egypt until he reaches Canaan, Walker insisted that "(RIGHTS) can never be secured or obtained by passiveness, inactivity, or indifference."[25] Rejecting the cooperative and compromising stance associated with both pietistic perfectionism and progressive accommodationism, he advocated confrontation with the status quo in the interest of full civil and human rights for African Americans. Walker symbolized the continuation of the type of black theology that James H. Cone discusses in connection with the black church freedom movement of the pre-Civil War years.[26]

The greatest proponent of religious nationalism was Henry M. Turner, the A.M.E. preacher who became a Reconstruction politician and later a bishop. Born in South Carolina in 1834, Turner was the chief advocate of emigration for African Americans between the Reconstruction years and World War I, believing that only a return to Africa would free his people from oppression at the hands of whites. Convinced that degradation "is against reason, against nature, against precedent and against God," and that "the nation as such has no disposition to give us manhood protection, Turner asserted in 1893, ten years after the Supreme Court nullified the Civil Rights Act of 1875, that "I have no hope in the future success of my race in our present situation."[27] According to Gayraud S. Wilmore, the mission of the black "church in Africa and the repatriation of Afro-Americans became the two great passions" of Turner's life. The view that Turner was both "a consummate politician" and "a theologians is impossible to refute, for he combined a concern for "social and economic intercourse between black America and Africa" with his belief that God was a black man who had allowed his people to be transported to the United States "to be equipped for a great missionary crusade in Africa."[28]

It is clear that the different social and political views of black preachers, in the period from roughly 1865 to 1900, were inseparable from their theological visions. To use terminology employed widely by contemporary liberation theologians, these preachers, despite their differences, believed that orthopraxis (right deeds) had to be a logical extension of orthodoxy (right belief).

The Black Church and Its Ministry: Deradicalized or Social-Action Oriented?

Gayraud S. Wilmore suggests that Booker T. Washington's address at the Atlanta Exposition helped trigger a shift in the ethos of the black church and its ministry. The point is that Washington's progressive accommodationist philosophy combined with the values of the emerging, conservative Christianity to drive black preachers and churches further away from radical, prophetic religion and theology in the period between 1895 and 1955:

> Washington's gradualism, while opposed by a few who were not dependent upon his influence for personal advancement, was adopted by most black preachers not only because they lacked the courage to fight back, but because it was consonant with the ethics of the white Christianity by which they were increasingly influenced. The picture of the nonviolent, self-effacing, patiently-suffering white Jesus held up by conservative evangelicals and revivalists at the turn of the century became for many black preachers the authoritative image of what it is like to be a Christian. That image provided irrefutable confirmation, supported by Scripture, of the wisdom and expediency of Washington's position.[29]

Wilmore's contention that most black preachers became "Bookerites" in the first half of the twentieth century is virtually impossible to disprove. The death of Henry M. Turner in 1915, followed by the revival of the Ku Klux Klan, the increase in racial violence, and the paralyzing effects of the Great Depression, left black churches frustrated, apathetic, and impotent. Many turned their attention inwardly, promoting their own institutional maintenance, and the at-large, social action-oriented, institutional church" became "the exception rather than the rule."[30] These developments put the lie to E. Franklin Frazier's contention that the black churches were "secularized in; that they, in the first half of the century, "lost their predominantly otherworldly outlook and began to focus attention upon the Negro's condition in this world."[31]

But the folk theology of hope and liberation did not completely fade. Some black preachers and churches were among the liberal Protestants who initiated trends in social gospel thought, a phenomenon which, in the period from roughly 1870 to 1918, sought to redeem American institutional life by applying the Biblical principles of love and justice to the social order.[32] Although most of the attention from scholars has been directed at white social gospelers such as Walter Rauschenbusch and Washington Gladden, it is clear that black social gospel prophets or prophetic pragmatists like Reverdy C. Ransom and Alexander Walters were more important in keeping alive the hope for African redemption and racial justice and harmony in America.

The folk theology, social advocacy, and political significance of the black church were embodied in Ramson, a Nanti-Bookeriten clergyman, who also became an A.M.E. bishop and "black social Christianity's foremost early spokesman."[33] Ransom, Sutton E. Griggs, J. Milton Waldron, and Francis J. Grinke were among those militant churchmen and black social gospel leaders who saw the need for organizational structures for protesting against racism, and they joined W. E. B. DuBois in 1905 as leading figures in the Niagara Movement. The most important black ideological precursor to the N.A.A.C.P.," the Niagara Movement, with a membership of some four hundred, "kept alive the tradition of virile protest" so long based in the church by clamoring for political rights, equal opportunities in economic life, free and compulsory education for children, and justice in the American courts.[34] While urging responsibilities upon their own people, such as the duty to vote, obey laws, and engage in policies of self-help, the black social gospelers held that America would never live up to its image as a Christian nation as long as whites arrogantly denied blacks full human rights:

We repudiate the monstrous doctrine that the oppressor should be the sole authority as to the rights of the oppressed. The Negro race in America, stolen, ravished, and degraded, struggling up through difficulties and oppression, needs sympathy and receives criticism; needs help and is given hindrance, needs protection and is given mob-violence, needs justice and is given charity, needs leadership and is given cowardice and apology, needs bread and is given a stone. This nation will never stand justified before God until these things are changed.[35]

Some of the same black preachers involved in the Niagara Movement emerged among the originators of the National Association for the Advancement of Colored People (N.A.A.C.P.) in 1909. Founded in New York to defend the civil rights of African Americans through litigation, this organization, from its origin, drew on the spiritual and material resources of the church and its ministry. The A.M.E. leader Reverdy Ransom, the A.M.E. Zion Bishop Alexander Walters, the Presbyterian minister Francis Grimke, the Baptist preacher J. Milton Waldron, and the black churchwomen Mary Church Terrell and Ida B. Wells-Barnett, all influenced by the social gospel, were among its founders and promoters.[36] They were all prophetic pragmatists who were concerned about the ways in which the gospel and the whole Biblical revelation spoke to the issues of human liberation and survival.

The rise of other civil rights agencies in the first half of the century also owed a lot to the social gospel tradition of the black church. The church figured prominently in the rise of the National Urban league in New York in 1910, an organization designed to assist African Americans, particularly in the periods of the Great Migration and economic depression, to adjust to the harsh realities of urbanization. In securing jobs, housing, and other material necessities for poor blacks, church supporters of the Urban League saw themselves as co-workers with God in improving the human condition. The same applied in the case of the Congress of Racial Equality (C.O.R.E.), which, after its origin in 1942, staged nonviolent sit-ins in Chicago.[37] The black theologian James H. Cone claims that the nonviolent and integrationist traditions of the C.O.R.E., traditions developed earlier in connection with the N.A.A.C.P., afforded a major intellectual and spiritual source for Martin Luther King, Jr., who later used the black church and its social gospel as the power base of his movement to move America from a racially segregated to a racially inclusive society.[38]

Black social gospelers, in a manner similar to white social gospel prophets like Josiah Strong and Washington Gladden, challenged the churches to become the conscience of the social order. Large black urban congregations, with resources for community uplift, were urged to assist the poverty-stricken, homeless, widowed, and orphaned. A few large urban congregations, such as R. C. Ransom's Institutional AME church in Chicago, H. H. Proctor's Congregational church in Atlanta, and the Abyssinian Baptist church of Adam Clayton Powell, Sr., in New York," writes Gayraud Wilmore, "became, in effect, social welfare agencies serving a broad spectrum of the needs of the burgeoning urban populations."[39] In putting forth their efforts, social gospel preachers like Ransom, Proctor, and Powell constantly faced, even in subtle ways, the challenges of black Christian fundamentalists, who felt that revival and personal conversion, not social and political reform, were the answer to America's racial dilemma.

The view in most circles is that prophetic pragmatists like Ransom, Griggs, Waldron, Grimke, Proctor, and Powell represented a minority tradition in the black church in the first half of the twentieth century. The dominant tradition was embodied in black fundamentalist Christianity, which perpetrated moralist and revivalism to the exclusion of a vibrant social gospel. It is also held that Martin Luther King, Jr. represented a shift away from this type of Christianity in the period from 1955 to 1968, a position strongly set forth by Gayraud Wilmore:

> If the period from the end of the First World War to the middle of the century saw growing disillusionment with the church because of a reactionary traditionalism, it must be said that it was the young Baptist minister Martin Luther King, Jr. who reversed that trend and gave new vitality and relevance to black Christianity in the United States.... King's contribution to the black revolution gave the lie to the allegation that black preachers were nothing but Uncle Toms and that Christianity was hopelessly out of tune with the times. Despite the fact that he was never able to muster the full power of the churches and received only token support from many of the most prestigious ministers, King nevertheless projected a new image of the church upon the nation and a new awareness of the possibilities inherent in black religion.[40]

It is more correct to say that King revitalized and built upon the social gospel tradition passed on by Ransom, Griggs, Waldron, and others. Like the black social gospel prophets before him, he implemented in practical ways the folk theology of hope and liberation that had roots in slave sources.[41] But unlike those prophets, King was the catalyst for the building of a strong inter-racial movement for freedom. King's ability to appeal to a sector of American society beyond the African American community is highlighted by Keith D. Miller, who notes that the civil rights leader "triumphed because, by adapting the traditions of the folk pulpit to a massive white audience, he became the greatest folk preacher of all."[42]

82

From Pietistic Perfectionism to Social Gospelism: Their Relevance for Black Theology

The discussion up to this point establishes that more than one tradition exists in connection with both the black preacher and the black church. This became abundantly clear in the period from 1865 to 1955, as competing views of religion and its relationship to life were set forth by pietistic perfectionists, prophetic pragmatists, progressive accommodationists, and religious nationalists. But all of these traditions have something to offer black theologians today as they seek to articulate visions of God in relationship to the continuing struggle against oppression.[43]

The pietistic perfectionists concern for the perfectibility of the person, as set forth in the thought of Daniel J. Russell, offers important insights. Because spiritual and moral values have declined so much in parts of the African American community, and because materialism is often appreciated more than the spiritual things of life, the idea of a personal conversion experience that leads to exemplary conduct in this life and a sense of eternal salvation in the afterlife has some merit. Unfortunately, contemporary black theology fails to sufficiently emphasize the need for personal transformation through conversion and sanctification.

The progressive accommodationist idea that there must be cooperation between African Americans and the status quo in the interest of a better society is worthy of consideration. Black theology has too often suggested, even subtlety, that African Americans, because of the very nature of their condition, always stand in conflict with the society and culture. The idea that religion must ultimately teach the oppressed to live in harmony with even the oppressor contains some truth, especially if both are to realize the true meaning of freedom. For all of its shortcomings, the progressive accommodationist ideal of "a harmonious, conflict-free society in which blacks can freely pursue their economic and political interests has some merit.[44]

But African Americans should not forget that the struggle for a just and inclusive society sometimes demands a reliance on the politics of confrontation. This is where the tradition of prophetic pragmatism in the black church offers some insights. Prophetic pragamatists from William E. Walker to Reverdy C. Ransom to Martin Luther King, Jr. remind us that the truly moral and religious person must always be prepared to engage in protest and even agitation against values, institutions, and practices that undermine human freedom and well-being. Prophetic pragmatism challenges black theology to never surrender the spirit of dissent and protest that was supremely exemplified in the lives and messages of Jesus and the ancient Hebrew prophets. Fortunately, contemporary black theology has not abandoned this dimension.[45]

The same can be said of the values of religious nationalism which have long found acceptance in certain quarters of the black church and its ministry. This tradition, as represented by Henry M. Turner, continued to challenge the black church later in the ideas and activities of Marcus Garvey and George A. McGuire. It challenges black preachers and churches today in Father George Stallings efforts to create a separate Catholic church that responds to the peculiar spiritual and ritualistic needs of people of African descent.[46] The values of self-esteem, self-reliance, and collective struggle within the race, which stand at the center of the tradition of religious nationalism, must continue to be significant in black theological reflection and discourse.

Put another way, black theology must become more eclectic and synthetic. It must draw from the best in the diverse traditions embodied by the black preacher and the black church from Reconstruction to the rise of Martin Luther King, Jr. and beyond, while combining those elements to form a theology that speaks to the convictions, yearnings, and hopes of the whole people. King, who became a great synthesizer of ideas, affords a model for how this might be accomplished.[47]

The ethos that has emerged out of the historic struggles of African American women must not be ignored in this developmental process for black theology. This point has been made consistently since the 1980's by black womanist theologians such as Delores S. Williams and Kelly Brown Douglas. James H. Cone is the only black male theologian who is taking seriously the historic experiences of African American women and their significance for black theology.[49] There are indeed black female representatives of the various traditions discussed in this chapter. Those representatives will be the focus of the next chapter, which explores the historic struggles of female preachers in the black church and the relevance and implications of those struggles for reshaping and re-conceptualizing black theology.

Endnotes

1. W. E. B. DuBois, "Litany at Atlanta," in *Darkwater: Voices from Within the Veil* (New York: Harcourt, Brace and Howe, 1920), p. 25.

2. Alfreda M. Duster, ed., *Crusade for Justice: The Autobiography of Ida B. Wells* (Chicago: the University of Chicago Press, 1970), p. 199.

3. Lewis V. Baldwin, *"Invisible" Strands in African Methodism: A History of the African Union Methodist Protestant and Union American Methodist Episcopal Churches, 1805-1980* (Metuchen, N.J.: The Scarecrow Press, Inc., 1983), p. 98.

4. *Ibid.*

5. This is most certainly suggested by Gayraud S. Wilmore, *Black Religion and Black Radicalism: An Interpretation of the Religious History of Afro-American People* (Maryknoll, N.Y.: Orbis Books, 1983), pp. 140-166.

6. Lerone Bennett, Jr., *Before the Mayflower: A History of the Negro in America. 1619-1964* (Baltimore: Penguin Books, 1966), pp. 379-382.

7. See Philip S. Foner, ed., *The Voice of Black America: Major Speeches by Blacks in the United States, 1797-1973,* 2 Vols., (New York: Capricorn Books, 1975), I, pp. 335-344; and Clarence E. Walker, *A Rock in a Weary Land: The African Methodist Episcopal Church During the Civil War and Reconstruction* (Baton Rouge: The Louisiana State University Press, 1982), p. 2.

8. Foner, ed., *The Voice of Black America*, I, pp. 343-344.

9. A brief but interesting and provocative discussion of how black churches increased their roles in addressing a range of problems during Reconstruction is afforded in E. Franklin Frazier, *The Negro Church in America* (New York: Schocken Books, 1964), pp. 31-46.

10. *Ibid.*, pp. 31-34.

11. *Ibid.*, pp. 34-38.

12. *Ibid.* This theology of uplift is treated at some length in Edward L. Wheeler, *Uplifting the Race: The Black Minister in the New South, 1865-1902* (Lanham, Md.: University Press of America, 1986), pp. 1-130.

13. Baldwin, *"Invisible" Strands in African Methodism*, p. 106; and Frazier, *The Negro Church in America*, pp. 38-42.

14. Frazier, *The Negro Church in America*, pp. 42-44; and Bennett, *Before the Mayflower*, p. 382.

15. Walker, *A Rock in a Weary Land*, pp. 2-3.

16. *Ibid.*, p. 2.

17. Herbert Aptheker, ed., *A Documentary History of the Negro in the United States: From the Reconstruction Years to the Founding of the N.A.A.C.P. in 1910*, 3 Vols (Secaucus, N.J.: The Citadel Press, 1972), II, pp. 551-571; and David N. Chalmers, *Hooded Americanism: The History of the Ku Klux Klan* (New York: New Viewpoints, 1981), pp. 8-21.

18. John Hope Franklin, *From Slavery to Freedom: A History of Negro Americans*, Fourth Edition (New York: Alfred A Knopf, 1974), p. 274.

19. Frazier, *The Negro Church in America*, p. 45.

20. The category of progressive accommodationists, a tradition that dates back at least as for as the late eighteenth century with the preacher-poet Jupiter Hammon, came from Robert M. Franklin, A Charisma and Conflict in Religious Belief and Political Activism in Black America," a lecture given at Vanderbilt University (7 April 1986), pp. 1-10; Robert M. Franklin, "Religious Belief and Political Activism in Black America: An Essay, *The Journal of Religious Thought*, 43, no. 2 (FallWinter, 1986-1987), pp. 63-72; and Lewis V. Baldwin, *To Make the Wounded Whole: The Cultural Legacy of Martin Luther King, Jr.* (Minneapolis: Fortress Press, 1992), pp. 8-19.

21. *A Short History of the Life of Rev. Dr. D. J. Russell: ExPresident of the Philadelphia and New Jersey Conference of the African Union Methodist Protestant Church* (Salem, N.J.: Press of Standard and Jerseyman, n.d.), pp. 3-5.

22. *A Short History of the Life of Rev. Dr. D. J. Russell*, pp. 913; and Daniel J. Russell, *History of the African Union Methodist Protestant Church* (Philadelphia: Union Star Book and Job Printing and Publishing House, 1920), pp. 1-4. The term "pietistic perfectionism" was commonly used in relation to Charles G. Finney and other revivalists in the nineteenth century, who emphasized the perfectibility of both the individual and the society. Continental Pietists like Philip J. Spener and August H. Francke stressed the same in the seventeenth and eighteenth century. But "pietistic perfectionism," or "Christian perfection," was often promoted, as in the case of Russell, without serious consideration

of the need for participation in social and political activism against racism and the structures of injustice.

23. Robert Franklin and Lewis V. Baldwin tell us that the key word for progressive accommodationists in the African American tradition is "cooperation" with the status quo, not "confrontation" with it. See Franklin, "Religious Belief and Political Activism," p. 64; and Baldwin, *To Make the Wounded Whole*, p. 9.

24. Franklin, "Religious Belief and Political Activism," p. 64; and Foner, ed., *The Voice of Black America*, I, pp. 607-612. Booker Washington urged his people to give up their struggle for civil rights, political power, and higher liberal arts education, while devoting their energies to industrial education and the acquisition of manual skills as a prerequisite to black freedom. His position has been referred to as "pressureless persuasion," "passive acceptance," "passive resignation," or "passive acquiescence." See Baldwin, *To Make the Wounded Whole*, p. 11.

25. Quoted in James M. Washington, *Frustrated Fellowship: The Black Baptist Ouest for Social Power* (Macon, Ga.: Mercer University Press, 1986), p. 120.

26. James H. Cone, *Liberation: A Black Theology* (Philadelphia and New York: J. B. Lippincott, 1970), p. 59; and Baldwin, *"Invisible" Strands in African Methodism*, p. 38.

27. Foner, ed., *The Voice of Black America*, I, pp. 591 and 598.

28. Wilmore, *Black Religion and Black Radicalism*, pp. 122-129.

29. *Ibid.*, p. 140.

30. Wilmore contends that "The de-radicalization of the black church ...was almost complete by the middle of this century." See *Ibid.*, pp. 136, 140, 161, and 165.

31. Frazier, *The Negro Church in America*, pp. 49-51.

32. Ronald C. White, Jr., *Liberty and Justice for All: Racial Reform and the Social Gospel, 1877-1925* (San Francisco: Harper & Row, Publishers, 1990), pp. 1-265; and Ralph E. Luker, *The Social Gospel in Black & White: American Racial Reform, 1885-1912* (Chapel Hill: The University of North Carolina Press, 1991), pp. 1-324.

33. Wilmore, *Black Religion and Black Radicalism*, p. 136; and Luker, *The Social Gospel in Black & White*, p. 175.

34. White, *Liberty and Justice for All*, p. 175; Luker, *The Social Gospel in Black & White*, pp. 254-256; Wilmore, *Black Religion and Black Radicalism*, pp. 136, 138, and 141-142, 170, and 229; Francis L. Broderick and August Meter, eds., *Negro Protest Thought in the Twentieth Century* (Indianapolis and New York: The Bobbs-Merrill Company, 1965), pp. 48-52.

35. Broderock and Meter, eds., *Negro Protest Thought in the Twentieth Century*, p. 51.

36. Wilmore, *Black Religion and Black Radicalism*, pp. 138 and 141; Luker, *The Social Gospel in Black & White*, pp. 261-262; and White, *Liberty and Justice for All*, pp. 177-182.

37. Wilmore, *Black Religion and Black Radicalism*, p. 142; and Bennett, *Before the Mayflower*, p. 395.

38. James H. Cone, "The Theology of Martin Luther King, Jr., in *Union Seminary Quarterly Review*, XL, no. 4 (1986), p. 22.

39. Wilmore, *Black Religion and Black Radicalism*, p. 160.

40. *Ibid.*, p. 174.

41. This point is emphasized in Baldwin, *To Make the Wounded Whole*, pp. 63-66.

42. Keith D. Miller, *Voice of Deliverance: The Language of Martin Luther King Jr. and Its Sources* (New York: The Free Press, 1992), p. 141.

43. A part of Martin Luther King, Jr.'s genius stemmed from his willingness to see some value in all of these traditions. See Baldwin, *To Make the Wounded Whole*, pp. 52-55.

44. Franklin, "Religious Belief and Political Activism," p. 64.

45. Cone, "The Theology of Martin Luther King, Jr.," pp. 26-36.

46. Laura B. Randolph, "What's Behind the Black Rebellion in the Catholic Church?," in *Ebony*, XLV, no. 1 (November, 1989), pp. 160-164; and Alayna A. Gaines, "Catholicism's Maverick: Out spoken Archbishop George A. Stallings, Jr.," in *Emerge*, VI, no. 6 (April, 1995), pp. 20-24.

47. Baldwin, *To Make the Wounded Whole*, pp. 52-55.

48. Delores S. Williams, "Womanist Theology: Black Women's Voices: A Language for the Spirit," *Christianity and Crisis*, 47, no. 3 (2 March 1987), pp. 66-70; Delores S. Williams, *Sisters in the Wilderness:*

The Challenge of Womanist God-Talk (Maryknoll, N.Y.: Orbis Books, 1993), pp. 1-239; and Kelly Brown Douglas, *The Black Christ* (MaryRnoll, N.Y.: Orbis Books, 1994), pp. 92-117.

49. See James H. Cone, *For My People: Black Theology and the Black Church -- Where Have We Been and Where Are We Going?* (Maryknoll, N.Y.: Orbis Books, 1984), pp. 122-139. Fleeting attention is devoted to the subject in Noel Leo Erskine, *King Among the Theologians* (Cleveland: The Pilgrim Press, 1994), pp. 159-171.

Chapter Four

Usurping Male Authority: Women and Ministry in the Black Church

But to my utter surprise there seemed to sound a voice which I thought I distinctly heard, and most certainly understand, which said to me, "Go preach the Gospel!" I immediately replied aloud, "No one will believe me." Again I listened, and again the same voice seemed to say -- "Preach the Gospel; I will put words in your mouth, and will turn your enemies to become your friends."

Jarena Lee[1]

At times, when theological arguments were invoked against the ordination of women, I shuttled between faith and inner doubt. These arguments carried the force of a two thousand-year tribal taboo and were so deeply embedded in the psyche....

Pauli Murray[2]

The struggle of African American women for the right to preach is almost as old as the black church in the United States. It began on a serious note in the early nineteenth century, and it continues today in a cultural milieu that has always been dominated by patriarchal structures. Throughout the long history of the black church, most of its constituents, male and female, have subscribed to narrow readings of scripture and tradition that deny women access to the ministry and other areas of leadership typically held by men.

The multitude of problems encountered by black female preachers in the black church over the last two centuries have not been seriously treated by scholars. This still holds true despite the vigorous assault made by black womanist thinkers on male domination in black church structures. This chapter highlights the historic struggle of African American women to achieve recognition as preachers and pastors in the black church. The ideas and circumstances which contributed to opposition to and support for black women in ministry will be carefully underscored.

Women Answering the Call to Preach: The Pre-Civil War Years

Black churches assumed different denominational forms from their origins in the late eighteenth and early nineteenth centuries. Most were Baptists and Methodists, but there were also Episcopalians, Presbyterians, and Catholics. Different approaches to organization, discipline, and polity existed within these institutional structures, and there was diversity at other levels, but most found common ground in the position they took toward the idea of women serving as preachers and pastors.

Perhaps the first black denomination to grapple seriously with the issue of women in ministry was the Union Church of Africans, a Methodist body that began in Wilmington, Delaware under the leadership of Peter Spencer and William Anderson in 1813.[3] This church apparently accepted women preachers from its beginning as a natural consequence of its "stress on congregational control and strong lay involvement," and also because Spencer and Anderson were under the strong influence of Quakers.[4] "Concerning women preaching," they wrote in one of their early Books of Discipline, "the Quaker friends have always spoken for us, that being their way, they shall always preach for us when they have a mind, and none but them." Lewis V. Baldwin notes that this attitude toward females in ministry grew out of the concept of religious freedom held by the Union Church of Africans:

> The position Spencer and his followers took regarding the place of women in the church is further illustrative of this idea of religious freedom. Spencer evidently did not feel that women should be confined exclusively to quiet roles in the background of church affairs. He may have been as vigorous as John Wesley, the father of Methodism, in affirming the spiritual freedom of women and their capacity for leadership in certain areas of church life. In the early Methodist movement of John Wesley women assumed roles as itinerants, group leaders, active visitors and callers, benefactresses, models of the Christian life for men and women alike, and even preachers. Although women in the Union Church of Africans undertook similar roles, there is no evidence that this policy was based on the Wesleyan model.[6]

But for all their stress on the right of women to preach the gospel, the male leaders of the Union Church of Africans did not escape the kind of socialization process that upheld male supremacy in the church and society. Baldwin further observes:

> But the early leaders of this church, including Spencer, were not willing to place women in all positions of authority and influence. Their understanding of the Bible, and their absorption into a male-dominated culture, kept them from being completely free of the concept of women's subordination. For example, women could not serve as trustees in the early Union Church of Africans, nor could they be lay elders, elder ministers,

and deacons. Even so, women seem to have been more visibly present in the Spencer movement than in the African Methodist movements led by Richard Allen and James Variek. Furthermore, in insisting that women had a place in the ministry of the church, the leaders of the early African Union Church were granting a privilege that was not so readily available to women in most black churches in that period. There is no question that Spencer's denomination was one of the first among black people to assert as a matter of principle and practice that women could and should be preachers.[7]

Despite the policy put in place by the Union Church of Africans, there is no extant record of a woman having applied for a license to preach in the pre-Civil War years. However, there were women like Mother Ferreby Draper, Mother Lydia Hall, Araminta Jenkins, and Annes Spencer, Peter Spencer's wife, who exhorted, taught religion, prayed for the sick, offered counseling and healing potions, and undertook other duties typically associated with ministry. These women had more influence among their fellow-church persons than some of the male preachers.[8] In their functions as strong spiritual forces in their church and community, they triggered memories of slave women who gained influence on the plantation as conjurers.

The struggles of women to earn the right to preach in the A.M.E. Church constitute some of the most interesting stories in the antebellum black church. Jarena Lee, born in New Jersey in 1783, personified those struggles. Converted in 1816 after a severe illness and attempted suicide, Lee immediately felt a call from God to undertake exhortation in the church. "For a few moments," she declared, "I had power to exhort sinners, and to tell of the wonders and of the goodness of Him who had clothed me with His salvation."[9] After another suicide attempt in 1820, Lee experienced sanctification, and by 1825 had been called to preach.

She shared her experience with Richard Allen, the A.M.E. founder and first bishop, who initially responded to her in typical male fashion:

> I now told him, that the Lord had revealed it to me, that I must preach the gospel. He replied, by asking, in what sphere I wished to move in? I said, among the Methodists. He then replied, that a Mrs. Cook, a Methodist lady, had also some time before requested the same privilege; who, it was believed, had done much good in the way of exhortation, and holding prayer meetings; and who had been permitted to do so by the verbal license of the preacher in charge at the time. But as to women preaching, he said that our Discipline knew nothing at all about it -- that it did not call for women preachers.[10]

Lee initially felt relieved by Allen's response, but later felt that she had been running away from God's call like Jonah. After her testimony at Bethel A.M.E. Church in Philadelphia some time later, Allen, who was present, "declared that he now knew that she was as truly called to preach as anyone."[11] Although Bishop Allen never overcame all of his reservations about women preachers, Lee was eventually licensed in the A.M.E. Church, and became a traveling evangelist, preaching in churches in Delaware, Maryland, Pennsylvania, New Jersey, and other parts of the Northeast. In her autobiographical account, "She described herself as the first female preacher of the First African Methodist Episcopal Church."[12]

Jarena Lee stood in the black church tradition of pietistic perfectionism, preaching the doctrine of sanctification or Christian perfection that stood at the core of much of nineteen century

American theology. She must be understood within the context of that time frame, when there was an Arminian emphasis on the work of the Holy Spirit which provided even women opportunities to use their spiritual gifts. Furthermore, Lee was obviously influenced by the growing stress on the freedom of the Christian to be experimental, and by reinterpretations of the Bible that came from white women like Phoebe Palmer. This explains the enthusiasm with which she used the Bible in defense of the woman's right to preach:

> Did not Mary first preach the risen Saviour, and is not the doctrine of the resurrection the very climax of Christianity -- hangs not all our hope on this, argued by St. Paul? Then did not Mary, a woman, preach the gospel? For she preached the resurrection of the crucified Son of God.... But some will say that Mary did not expound the Scripture, therefore, she did not preach, in the proper sense of the term. To this I reply, it may be that the term preach in those primitive times, did not mean exactly what it is now made to mean; perhaps it was a great deal more simple then than it is now -- if it were not, the unlearned fishermen could not have preach the gospel at all, as they had no learning.[13]

Julia A. J. Foote, born in New York in 1823, had experiences similar to Lee's in the A.M.E. Church. After experiencing holiness, she exhorted in homes until she had a vision in which she was compelled to preach the gospel. "I had always been opposed to the preaching of women," she declared, "and had spoken against it though, I acknowledge, without foundation." "This rose before me like a mountain," she continued, "and when I thought of the difficulties they had to encounter, both from professors and non-professors, I shrank back and cried,

"Lord, I cannot go!"[14] But Foote, also a representative of pietistic perfectionism, overcame her doubts and decided to preach, a decision that brought opposition from fellow A.M.E.s and that led to her excommunication.[15] Her appeals were ignored, but she devoted herself nonetheless to traveling and preaching, primarily in New York.

Jarena Lee's and Julia Foote's stubbornness in pursuing their right to preach helps explain why the question of licensing women became so critical in the A.M.E. Church in the 1840s. Foote actually attended the A.M.E. General Conference in Philadelphia in 1844, where a resolution calling for the licensing of women was introduced and then shouted down. In 1848, at the next General Conference, A.M.E.s voted in favor of licensing women, a move that was heavily criticized by Bishop Daniel Payne and his delegates.[16] Payne expressed a view that was quite common among males and females in the black church generally at that time:

> To license women preachers would introduce distractions into the annual conferences.... Such a course as this, is calculated to break up the sacred relations which women bear to their husbands and children, by sending them forth as itinerant preachers, wandering from place to place, to the utter neglect of their household duties and obligations.... Such a course is unwarranted by the word of God, and the whole history of the church does not furnish a single instance where the legislative body of a church has ever licensed women preach.[17]

Julia Foote's perseverance reaped a beautiful harvest. After many years of preaching, she was ordained a deacon in the New York Annual Conference of the A.M.E. Zion Church in 1884 by Bishop JamesWalker Hood, the very first woman deacon in the history of that denomination.[18] Zilpha Elaw was equally determined in her fight to secure recognition as a preacher. Born near Philadelphia in 1790, this African American woman received the call to preach in the Methodist Episcopal Church (M.E.) in 1820. Despite opposition from her own husband and other blacks in her church, Elaw became a powerful preacher and evangelist, spreading the word throughout the North-eastern United States and in England.[19] Interestingly enough, Elaw was representative of the tradition of prophetic pragmatism in the black church, for she attacked both the racism of white Christians and the sexism so pervasive in the churches. She proudly pointed to Biblical figures like Phoebe and Priscilla, who preached under the "extraordinary directions of the Holy Spirit, in advancing her defense of the woman's right to ascend the pulpit and proclaim God's word."[20]

The struggles of female preachers in the black churches paralleled in some ways those of African Americans against the structures of white racism. In the Methodist, Baptist, Presbyterian, Episcopal, and Catholic Churches, the dominant view was that women were created to function in the private sphere; to be good mothers and to take care of the home. Unable to break through this maze of tradition, some black women broke away from established black churches and became preachers and spiritual leaders in their own religious movements. Rebecca Cox Jackson is a case in point. Born in Philadelphia in 1795, she broke away from the A.M.E. Church, in which she encountered fierce resistance, and in 1837 joined a New York-based Shaker community, a community in which women held prominent leadership roles. A personification of the pietistic perfectionist tradition, she insisted on preaching and ultimately founded "the first African American community of the United Society of Believers in Christ's Second Appearing (Shakers)."[21]

The position of women preachers in black churches was not changed dramatically by the emergence of females generally to the forefront of American religion. Few black churches were prepared in the pre-Civil War years to take the kind of steps that the American revivalist Charles G. Finney took with regard to women. Finney's insistence on female participation at all levels of church life was foreign to black Christians who had accepted uncritically the Victorian idea of separate spheres for men and women.[22]

And Your Daughters Shall Prophesy: Fighting the Same Battles, 1865-1954

The changes in the social and political situation of African Americans that followed the Emancipation Proclamation and the Civil War did not translate into a radical shift in views regarding women in ministry in the black church. Black females who asserted their calls to preach found themselves fighting the same battles that their spiritual foremothers had fought. Traditionalists who upheld female subordination based on scripture and custom in the church continued to dominate numerically and in terms of the shaping of policy concerning female preachers. Egalitarians, who asserted the essential equality of men and women in the ministry of the church, remained as scarce as hen's teeth.

Much of the debate and controversy concerning female preachers continued to rage in the A.M.E. Church. Some of the issues came to a head in 1872, when Harriet A. Baker, born in Maryland in 1829, announced her intentions to preach. Fellow A.M.E.s greeted her with the claim that "God did not intend women to preach. However, by 1875, resistance to her intentions had waned to the point that the church sanctioned her right to proclaim the word.[23]

Extensive discussions of women's ministry took place among A.M.E.s in the 1880s. After much debate at the General Conference of 1884 in Baltimore, A.M.E.s "permitted the licensing of women ministers as evangelists who could only hold special services but did not consider the issue of women's ordination." The decision that women would not be accepted as pastors virtually assured a continuation of the debates, especially since two females, Sarah A. Hughes of North Carolina and Margaret Wilson of New Jersey, were forced to relinquish the pastorates they had been given earlier by their annual conferences.[24]

In 1885, the issue of women's ordination surfaced in powerful ways with the A.M.E. Bishop Henry M. Turner, whose position on the role of women in the church close approximated Frederick Douglass's stance on the rights of women generally. Turner ordained Sarah Hughes, boasting that "he had done something that had not been done in 1,500 years -- that was the ordination of a woman to the office of deaconess in the church, but he trusted that it would redound to the honor and glory of God. That action provoked a series of attacks on Turner, and the controversy was aired in the pages of the *Christian Recorder* and the *A.M.E. Church Review*, two church periodicals.[25] The validity of Hughes's ordination was rejected by the A.M.E. General Conference in 1888 on the grounds that it could not be defended by the Bible, and Bishops were forbidden by resolution to ordain women as deacons and elders.[26]

The issue appears not to have been this emotionally charged in other black churches. In 1876, the A.M.E. Zion Church voted to "strike out the word 'male' in the Discipline," a move that was consistent with its stress on strong lay involvement at all levels. Mary J. Small was licensed to preach in 1892, ordained a deacon in 1895, and ordained an elder by Bishop Calvin C. Pettey in 1898, becoming the first woman to hold such a position in the denomination. In 1894, Julia A.J. Foote was ordained a deacon by Bishop James W. Hood, and, after transferring from the New York to the New Jersey Annual Conference, she received ordination as an elder under Bishop Alexander Walters in 1900.[27] These developments most certainly raised the eyebrows of male chauvinists in the A.M.E. Zion Church, but they seem to have occurred with little fanfare. In fact, the A.M.E. Zion Church is said to have been the first black denomination to grant "full clergy rights" to women.[28]

Churches that stemmed from the work of Peter Spencer, most notably the A.U.M.P. and U.A.M.E. bodies, continued their traditions of licensing females as preachers. The dearth of vigorous male leadership in these denominations often necessitated the use of women as pastors, so practical considerations in such cases outweighed any opposition that might have arisen out of a concern for tradition and Biblical teachings. Lydia Archie of the A.U.M.P. Church gained a wide reputation as a preacher and pastor within her denomination during the last two decades of the nineteenth century, receiving recognition in reputable Wilmington newspapers like *The Evening Journal.*[29]

The most widely known African American female preacher in the M.E. Church was Amanda Berry Smith. Born in 1837, she stands as an excellent example of the kind of female preacher who refused to be curtailed by her church's stance against women's ordination. Though never ordained, Smith, yet another representative of pietistic perfectionism, preached at holiness camp meetings in parts of the United States and Britain, and engaged in evangelistic activities in Africa and India.[30] Convinced that the call of God was much more significant than any confirmation that came through the church via ordination, she was by far the most important female preacher in her church in the late nineteenth century.

The early years of the twentieth century did bring some hope for more gender inclusiveness in the ministry of the black church. Black women such as Neeley Terry and Lucy P. Farrow emerged as strong preachers in the holiness movement, recalling the work of earlier figures like Jarena Lee and Amanda B. Smith.[31] The beginnings of Pentecostalism in Los Angeles in 1906, as an outgrowth of the Holiness movement, afforded other opportunities for female leadership in ministry. The same can be said of other sectarian movements that originated, such as the spiritual Churches, and also religious cults that arose in large black urban areas in the North.[32] These movements, evoking memories of Gnosticism and Manichaeism in the ancient church, emerged outside the confines of established religious culture and tended to break with that culture on the roles of women in religion. In other words, they tended to be more open to the idea of women as preachers and pastors. However, this tendency had reversed itself by World War II with the Holiness and Pentecostal movements, for by that time they had emerged out of cultural isolation and had taken on an attitude toward women in ministry that coincided with that of established religious institutions.

The renewed struggle against racism in the early years of the twentieth century, symbolized mostly in the social gospel tradition as promoted by prophetic pragmatists in the black church, did not embrace the issues of gender exclusiveness in the church and society. Even so, women continued to perform ministerial tasks, often behind the scenes, but some became great public speakers, preachers, and even pastors. Among such figures were Florence S. Randolph, who served successfully as pastor of the Wallace Chapel A.M.E. Zion Church in Summit, New Jersey (1925-1946); Mary G. Evans, a powerful evangelist in the A.M.E. Church; Clara Wright of the A.U.M.P. Church; Mother Rosa A. Horn and Bishop Ida Robinson of the Holiness and Pentecostal Churches; Quinceila Whitlow and F. E. Redwine of the Christian Methodist Episcopal Church (C.M.E.); and Mother Leafy Anderson of the Eternal Life Spiritualist Church of Chicago.[33]

These women were not influenced heavily by trends in the social gospel movement. They tended to be products of the traditions of pietistic perfectionism and progressive accommodationism. Even so, their struggles for proper acceptance and recognition in the church paved the way for the next generation of female clergy who made important contributions to the modern phase of the civil rights movement.

Responding to New Challenges: A New Day for Women in Ministry

The civil rights movement of the 1950s and 1960s helped bring the issue of women's rights to the forefront of America's social and political agenda. Although Martin Luther King, Jr. and the other male clergy, who gained wide public recognition as leaders of the movement, devoted their time, energies, and resources to overcoming racial barriers in the society, their failure to properly acknowledge the contributions of women to the crusade brought attention to the problem of gender exclusiveness. King and his fellow ministers in the Southern Christian Leadership Conference (S.C.L.C.), the organization brought into being to give Christian discipline and continuity to protest activities, did not respond well to female leadership in the movement.[34] Septima Clark, who worked with the educational wing of the S.C.L.C. in the 1960s, has reported that

> Like other black ministers, Dr. King didn't think too much of the way women could contribute. But working in a movement, he changed the lives of so many people that it was getting to the place where he would have to see that women are more than sex symbols.... But in those days, of course, in the black church men were always in charge. It was just the way things were.[35]

Ella Baker and Dorothy Cotton, who also worked closely with the S.C.L.C., related similar impressions regarding King and other ministers in the movement. "I did have a decision-making role," declared Cotton on one occasion, "but I'm also very conscious of the male chauvinism that existed. Black preachers are some of the most chauvinistic of them all."[36] Clark, Baker, and Cotton challenged, in their own ways, "the male-dominated charismatic leadership models represented by King and other ministers, mainly because they believed that it stifled the kind of creative contributions that women could make to the freedom cause. These women opted instead for what Baker called "group centered leadership," a more democratic model that would have allowed for stronger roles on the part of female clergy and laity.[37]

Some female ministers transcended the proscribed roles set for them by black male preachers and made tremendous contributions to the civil rights movement. Cases in point are Pauli Murray and Willie Barrow. Born in 1910 in Baltimore, Murray, the first female priest of the African American Episcopal Church, and a product of the tradition of prophetic pragmatism, was arrested and fined as early as March, 1940 for refusing to obey laws upholding bus segregation. Murray's book, *States' Laws on Race and Color* (1951), a comprehensive treatment of segregation laws, was called by Supreme Court Justice Thurgood Marshall "The Bible for civil rights lawyers working against segregation."[38] Influenced by the nonviolent philosophies of Nohandas K. Gandhi and Martin Luther King, Jr., Murray actively protested racial segregation. But her insistence of the liberation of women in ministry, in the movement, and in society put her somewhat at odds with Martin Luther King, Jr.[39]

Willie Barrow, born in 1924 in Burton, Texas, joined King, Jesse Jackson, and other male preachers in the crusade for civil rights in the 1960s. In 1969, Jackson and Barrow led a campaign in Chicago to highlight the problem of hunger. Barrow, an associate pastor in the Vernon Park Church of God in Chicago, also worked as Director of Special Projects for Operation Breadbasket of the S.C.L.C., a program set in motion by King and other ministers to address economic problems faced by African Americans. After Jesse Jackson organized Operation P.U.S.H. in 1971, to advance economic opportunity for the poor, Barrow became one of its most active supporters. In the mid-seventies, she served as the first female national vice president of P.U.S.H., and in 1984, when Jackson ran for President of the United States, she served for a time as president of the organization. From 1986 to 1989, she became the P.U.S.H. president on a more permanent basis.[40] Also a proponent of prophetic pragmatism, Barrow, much like Pauli Murray, represented the beginnings of a new trend in the preaching tradition of black women.

The flowering of the women's movement in the 1960s and 1970s attracted black female preachers who had been inspired and influenced by the civil rights movement. Pauli Murray was one such person. Like a growing number of black women in ministry, she saw clearly the intimate connection between racism and sexism. The women's movement forced many black female preachers to become more assertive about their right to preach and pastor in black churches. Lynn Norment has made the point in words poignant enough for extended quotation:

> In marbled sanctuaries on city streets and in tiny churches on dusty country roads, a different kind of voice is heard preaching the gospel these days -- the voice of an increasing number of female pastors. Despite opposition from some hard-line male clergymen who still have difficulty accepting women in the pulpit, some Black women are not deterred from leading their own congregations. Bolstered by women's liberation and female assertiveness at home and on the job, they are quietly but persistently nudging for equal opportunities in God's house. They want to serve in a higher capacity than missionary, musician, choir director, Sunday school teacher, usher, youth leader or church secretary -- the "traditional" church roles for women.[41]

All the more important is the fact that the growing number of female preachers and pastors in black churches are bringing new ideas and insights to the pulpit. One contemporary black church historian has noted that "one of the emerging realities of today's church is the availability of intelligent, extremely well-qualified young women offering themselves for church leadership roles":

> They are women who are tough-minded, deeply committed, internally secure and deeply-rooted in their faith, and the church is going to have to recognize that they are a tremendous resource to be utilized.... God in Providence didn't make decisions based on a person's sex, and I'm sure he won't when we die either.[42]

Foremost among the new ideas of black female preachers and pastors is the sense that ministry in the black church must become more inclusive, far-reaching, and relevant. They fully understand that ministry and mission are the function of the whole church, clergy and laity, and that they are not to be monopolized by persons who operate out of egoism, false piety, and a hunger for exhibitionism. At a time when too many black male preachers are abusing their power and violating the public trust, women in ministry may well be the key to a revitalized black church.[43]

The testimonies of black women in ministry since the 1970s are the best source for understanding the new type of thinking that is penetrating the consecrated walls of black churches. L. Emma Cables, an ordained deacon in the U.A.N.E. Church, expressed this point of view in 1974: "I see no reason why anyone should consider it unusual for a woman to be a minister. Women do a great deal of important church work of many kinds; and being a minister and a preacher most certainly should be one of them."[44] I always thought that's what God wanted me to do," stated the Reverend Tallulah Fisher Williams of Chicago concerning her ministry in 1981. "I wasn't really aware that women weren't supposed to be ministers, so I didn't anticipate any problems."[45] The Reverend Dorothy L. Pearson of Columbia, South Carolina offered a different perspective, noting that "I feel that through God I have helped pave the way for upcoming female ministers who have been called by God to pastor."[46]

Perhaps unprecedented is the rise, over the last two decades, of the black female preacher-intellectual who is more gifted and equipped for a vital ministry than many black male clergymen. This is most certainly the case with Prathia L. Hall, a Baptist pastor in Philadelphia, who, according to one source, "combines the best scholarship with keenly precise Biblical interpretation and passionately persuasive delivery." Of equal ability and intellect is Renita J. Weems, an A.M.E. preacher, Ph.D. in Old Testament and Hebrew Languages, and professor at Vanderbilt University Divinity School, who makes the Bible "come alive to town and gown." Also important in this regard is Ella P. Mitchell, one of the "Mothers in the Gospel ministry." Mitchell, a Baptist minister who is well trained and published, lectures and preaches throughout the country.[47] A number of other contemporary black female preachers of considerable training and ability also function throughout the United States, some of whom were recognized by *Ebony Magazine* in November, 1997.

Some of these black women in ministry are representative of the tradition of prosperity positivism in the black church, a tradition that emphasizes the power of positive thinking, esoteric rituals and knowledge, and the prosperous life.[48] This tradition, initially shaped by Mother Leafy Anderson and other female and male preachers in spiritualist churches at the turn of this century, and later reinforced by the ministry of the Reverend Frederick J. Eikerenkoetter (Rev. Ike), is indeed growing as rapidly among female as among male preachers. The current efforts of the Reverend Jeanne D. Cotton to instill self-esteem and positive thinking at all levels of black church life are definitely reflective of this tradition.[49] Perhaps more representative of the tradition is the Reverend Johnnie Coleman, the founder and pastor of Christ Universal Temple in Chicago, a congregation consisting of some 12,000. Coleman's "gospel of material prosperity," which promises "health, prosperity, and success," suggests something of the wave of the future as far as women in ministry is concerned.[50]

The Preaching Tradition of Black Women: A Source for Reshaping Black Theology

Black theology as an intellectual phenomenon stands in serious need of reconstruction. Perhaps the best source for that process is the preaching tradition forged through time by black women in ministry. Up to this point, black male theologians, with few exceptions, have totally ignored the black female preaching tradition as a source of theological reflection and discourse.[51] The situation is quite different for black womanist theologians, who make the historic experiences of African American women their point of departure for doing theology.

The preaching traditions of black women afford several lessons that are useful for shaping a theology that speaks to African Americans collectively. One lesson involves the need to reinterpret scripture in liberating ways, rather than in a fashion that enslaves one spiritually and intellectually. Historic patterns of thought which have long excluded women from ministry in the black church have been grounded in narrow interpretations of the Bible. As an oppressed people, black Americans can no longer afford to interpret the Bible in ways that degrade and limit the abilities and potential of women. This is all the more important given our consistent assault on the ways in which whites have always used scripture to justify and sanction black oppression.

Second, the history of black women in ministry compels us to rethink our understanding of the church and culture. The black male theologian Hycel B. Taylor is right in saying that "the church must undergo a cultural adjustment to accept the inevitable increase of women ministers." Taylor notes that "Even in those denominations that do ordain women, they are still treated as inferior to males." "Many women who have studied under me," he adds, "often come back and tell me the problems they encounter. They are given the smallest churches, and they rarely get the same remunerations as male pastors."[52] A serious reconceptualization of the church and culture, encouraged by the scholarship of theologians can lead African Americans beyond this internal problem in the black church.

Finally, the black female preaching tradition forces us to redefine our sense of the workings of God's revelation through the Holy Spirit. The question of how the divine presence is revealed today in the everyday lives of males and females is perennially relevant for the black church. The point is that God's revelation, as the lives and testimonies of women preachers from Jarena Lee to Johnnie Coleman suggest, transcends the Bible to include what God is saying to us now. The belief in the power of the Holy Spirit to speak directly to persons dates back to the slaves, and is therefore a tradition that the black church and black theology need to recapture.

Women: Co-laborers in the Gospel of Jesus Christ – A Biblical Mandate

The Apostle Paul's mission allowed him to interact with a number of women who were actively engaged in ministry. In Romans 16:1-15 Paul lists eight women by name who served either as a deaconess or prophetess when they labored for the Lord:

Phebe, verses 1-2

Priscilla, Aquila verse 3

Mary, verse 6

Tryphena, verse 12

Tryphosa, verse 12

Persis, verse 12

Julia, verse 15

Verse 12 suggests that they labored in the ministry of the Word. 2 Corinthians 5:17 and Galatians 3:28 assure believers that our position in Christ guarantees us that everything is new in Christ. Now all races, classes, and sexes are one in Christ and are equal in rights and privileges. Women have a biblical mandate to serve in the ministry. If anyone would honestly look into the Word of God and read the actual deeds, acts and historical involvement of women in the New Testament all questions would end. The New Testament lists powerful examples of Jesus' acceptance of women and His revolutionary message about gender equality.[53] Jesus overthrew many centuries of Jewish law and customs. He consistently treated men and women as equals. He replaced several Old Testament laws and rules which promoted and validated gender inequality. His revolutionary acts shattered the traditional views of His day and replaced them with a new all inclusive, holistic and liberated Gospel.[54]

In Mark 5:25-34 Jesus completely ignores traditional laws concerning ritual impurity and cured a woman who suffered from menstrual bleeding for twelve years. Tradition said that it was a transgression for any man to talk to a woman other than his wife or children; yet, when Jesus healed her, she felt it and so did He. Luke 13:16 gives an example of a woman who had a spirit of infirmity for 18 years was healed. Afterwards, Jesus called her a daughter of Abraham; a clear indication that women and men are equal in His sight.

Acts 2:1-21 is another example of how women were actively involved in ministry. On the day of Pentecost, the Holy Spirit entered both men and women. In verse 27, Peter quotes a verse from the prophet Joel that talks about sons and daughters; verse 18 talks about men and women. In Acts 9:36 Paul refers to a certain disciple named Tabitha who was a woman full of good works and alms deeds. The name Tabitha means Dorcas in Greek. Acts 21:9 refers to the four daughters of Philip the evangelist. These four daughters are listed as prophetesses (Acts 21:9).

Women have always had a special place in the Old Testament and New Testament ministry. Loren Cunningham and David Joel Hamilton bring a fresh, yet profound insight into a prolific ministry for women today.[55] The challenges that they make and the questions that they raise demand an answer. Church leaders cannot afford to continue with business-as-usual and continue to side-step, ignore and by-pass the gifts that women bring to the table in 2004. The needs of the church today are simply enormous – yes the harvest is truly plenteous and the laborers are few.

There are other concerns that black theologians must address as they interpret the traditions of the black church and its ministry in relation to the issues of black liberation and survival. These concerns are the focus of attention in the chapter that follows.

Endnotes

1. Rosemary R. Ruether and Rosemary S. Keller, *Women and Religion in America, Volume I: The Nineteenth Century* (San Francisco: Harper & Row, Publishers, 1981), p. 212.

2. Pauli Murray, *The Autobiography of a Black Activist, Feminist, Lawyer, Priest, and Poet* (Knoxville: The University of Tennessee Press, 1987), p. 430.

3. The only solid works on the history of these churches and their leadership are Lewis V. Baldwin, *"Invisible" Strands in African Methodism: A History of the African Union Methodist Protestant and Union American Methodist Episcopal Churches, 1805-1980* (Metuchen, N.J.: Scarecrow Press, 1983), pp. 1-241; and Lewis V. Baldwin, *The Mark of a Man: Peter Spencer and the African Union Methodist Tradition* (Lanham, Md.: University Press of America, 1987), pp. 1-87.

4. Baldwin, *The Mark of a Man*, p. 17.

5. *The Discipline of the African Union Church in the United States of America and Elsewhere*, Third Edition Enlarged (Wilmington, Del.: Porter & Eckel, 1852), p. 100; Baldwin, *"Invisible" Strands in African Methodism*, p. 63; and Baldwin, *The Mark of a Man*, pp. 16-17.

6. Baldwin, *The Mark of a Man*, pp. 16-17.

7. *Ibid.* Elder Ministers were the highest ranking clergy in the Union Church of Africans, because Spencer and Anderson rejected bishops who, as they saw it, undermined the democratic and congregational function of other Methodist Churches. See Baldwin, *"Invisible" Strands in African Methodism*, pp. 48-51.

8. Baldwin, *"Invisible" Strands in African Methodism*, p. 63.

9. Jarena Lee, *Religious Experiences and Journal of Mrs. Jarena Lee, Giving an Account of Her Call to Preach the Gospel* (Philadelphia: Published by the Author, 1849), p. 8.

10. *Ibid.*, p. 14-15; and Ruether and Keller, *Women and Religion in America*, pp. 212-213.

11. Larry G. Murphy, et. al., eds., *Encyclopedia of African American Religions* (New York: Garland Publishing, Inc., 1993), p. 452.

12. *Ibid.*

13. Ruether and Keller, *Women and Religion in America*, p. 214.

14. Murphy, et. al., eds., *Encyclopedia of African American Religions*, p. 274; and William L. Andrews, ed., *Sisters of the Spirit: Three Black Women's Autobiographies of the Nineteenth Century* (Bloomington, Ind.: Indiana University Press, 1986), p. 201.

15. Murphy, et. al., eds., *Encyclopedia of African American Religions*, p. 274.

16. *Ibid.*; and Clarence E. Walker, *A Rock in a Weary Land: The African Methodist Episcopal Church During the Civil War and Reconstruction* (Baton Rouge, La.: Louisiana State University Press, 1982), pp. 25-26.

17. Walker, *A Rock in a Weary Land*, pp. 25-26.

18. Murphy, et. al., eds., *Encyclopedia of African American Religions*, p. 274.

19. Andrews, ed., *Sisters of the Spirit*, pp. 51-160; and Murphy, et. al., eds., *Encyclopedia of African American Religions*, pp. 248-249.

20. Murphy, et. al., eds., *Encyclopedia of African American Religions*, pp. 248-249.

21. *Ibid.*, p. 390; Jean M. Humez, *Gifts of Power: The Writings of Rebecca Jackson. Black Visionary, Shaker Eldress* (Amherst, Mass.: University of Massachusetts Press, 1981), pp. 1-368; and Richard E. Williams, *Called and Chosen: The Story of Mother Rebecca Jackson and the Philadelphia Shakers* (Metuchen, N.J.: The Scarecrow Press, 1981), pp. 1-179. For an important primary source, see Rebecca Cox Jackson, *The Life and Writings of Rebecca Jackson, Senior, Commonly Called Mother Rebecca, Being Her Witness and Testimony Copied from Her Own Handwriting* (Cleveland: Western Reserve Historical Society, 1877).

22. William G. McLoughlin, *Revivals, Awakenings. and Reform: An Essay on Religion and Social Change in America, 1607-1977* (Chicago: University of Chicago Press, 1978), p. 124.

23. Bettye Collier-Thomas, *Daughters of Thunder: Black Women Preachers and Their Sermons, 1850-1979* (San Francisco: Jossey-Bass Publishers, 1998), p. 71.

24. Stephen W. Angell, *Bishop Henry McNeal Turner and African American Religion in the South* (Knoxville: The University of Tennessee Press, 1992), p. 181.

25. *Ibid.*, p. 182.

26. *Ibid.*, p. 184.

27. William J. Walls, *The African Methodist Episcopal Zion Church: Reality of the Black Church* (Charlotte: A.M.E. Zion Publishing House, 1993), pp. 111-112.

28. Collier-Thomas, *Daughters of Thunder*, p. 101.

29. *The Evening Journal*, Wilmington, Delaware (25 August 1890), p. 3; Russell, *History of the African Union Methodist Protestant Church*, p. 51; and Baldwin, *"Invisible" Strands in African Methodism*, p. 106-107.

30. Ruether and Keller, *Women and Religion in America*, pp. 18-23.

31. Gayraud S. Wilmore, *Black Religion and Black Radicalism: An Interpretation of the Religious History of Afro-American People* (Maryknoll, N.Y.: Orbis Books, 1983), pp. 152-153.

32. Joyce White, Women in the Ministry," in *Essence*, 7 (November, 1976), pp. 62-63, 104, 107, and 109; Collier-Thomas, *Daughters of Thunder*, pp. 173-207; Celia T. Marcelle and Catherine J. Robinson, eds., *Black Women in the Church: Historical Highlights & Profiles* (Pittsburgh: Magna Graphics, Inc., 1986), pp. 1-127; Hans A. Baer, *The Spiritual Movement: A Religious Response to Racism* (Knoxville: The University of Tennessee Press, 1984), p. 21; and Claude F. Jacobs and Andrew J. Kaslow, *The Spiritual Churches of New Orleans: Origins, Beliefs, and Rituals of an African-American Religion* (Knoxville: The University of Tennessee Press, 1991), pp. 2, 19, 31, and 33.

33. Collier-Thomas, *Daughters of Thunder*, pp. 101-220; Baer, *The Black Spiritual Movement*, pp. 18-21 and 119; and Baldwin, *"Invisible" Strands in African Methodism*, pp. 174-175.

34. James H. Cone, *Martin & Malcolm & America: A Dream or a Nightmare* (New York: Orbis Books, 1991), pp. 273-280.

35. Cynthia Stokes Brown, ed., *Ready from Within: Septima Clark and the Civil Rights Movement* (New Jersey: Africa World Press, Inc., 1990), pp. 78-79.

36. Quoted in Adam Fairclough, *To Redeem the Soul of America: The Southern Christian Leadership Conference and Martin Luther King, Jr.* (Athens: The University of Georgia Press, 1987), pp. 49-50.

37. These models are treated at some length in Lewis V. Baldwin, *There is a Balm in Gilead: The Cultural Roots of Martin Luther King,*

Usurping Male Authority:
Women and Ministry in the Black Church

Jr. (Minneapolis: Fortress Press, 1991), pp. 269-270; and Carol Mueller, "Ella Baker and the Origins of 'Participatory Democracy'," in Vicki L. Crawford, et. al., eds., *Women in the Civil Rights Movement: Trailblazers and Torchbearers, 1941-1965* (New York: Carlson Publishing, Inc., 1990), pp. 60-65.

38. Murray, *The Autobiography of a Black Activist*, pp. 138-149; and Murphy, et. al., eds., *Encyclopedia of African American Religions*, p. 518.

39. Murray, *The Autobiography of a Black Activist*, pp. 232, 307, 383, and 417.

40. Murphy, et. al., eds., *Encyclopedia of African American Religions*, p. 72.

41. Lynn Norment, "In the Male Domain of Pastoring: Women Find Success in the Pulpit," in *Ebony*, 37, no. 1 (November, 1981), p. 99.

42. *Ibid.*

43. *Private Interview* with Lewis V. Baldwin, Vanderbilt University, Nashville, Tennessee (11 August 1998).

44. Quoted in Baldwin, *The Mark of a Man*, p. 53.

45. Interestingly enough, the Reverend Tallulah F. Williams had a very unique understanding of ministry even when she and I were classmates at Garrett-Evangelical Theological Seminary in Evanston, Illinois in the late 1970s. She is currently a District Superintendent in the United Methodist Church in Illinois, overseeing a number of congregations. See Norment, "In the Male Domain of Pastoring," p. 100.

46. *Ibid.*

47. "15 Greatest Black Women Preachers," in *Ebony*, LIII, no. 1 (November, 1997), pp. 102, 104, and 112. Also see Renita J. Weems, *Battered Love: Marriage, Sex, and Violence in the Hebrew Prophets* (Minneapolis: Fortress Press, 1995), pp. 1147; Ella P. Mitchell, *Those Preachin' Women: Sermons by Black Women Preachers* (Valley Forge, Pa.: Judson Press, 1985), pp. 1-126; Ella P. Mitchell, *Those Preaching Women: More Sermons by Black Women Preachers*, Vol II (Valley Forge: Judson Press, 1985), pp. 1-109; and Ella P. Mitchell, *Women: To Preach or Not to Preach: 21 Outstanding Black Preachers Say Yes!* (Valley Forge, Pa.: Judson Press, 1991), pp. 1-144.

48. Hans Baer refers to this tradition as Thaumaturgical Manipulationism. See Hans A. Baer and Merrill Singer, *African-American*

Religion in the Twentieth Century: Varieties of Protest and Accommodation (Knoxville: The University of Tennessee, 1992), pp. 179-213.

49. See Jeanne D. Cotton, *Getting It Together: You. Life, and Living* (Lanham, Ed.: University Press of America, 1995), vii93. See especially the Foreword by Lewis V. Baldwin.

50. "15 Greatest Black Women Preachers," p. 112; Baer and Singer, *African-American Religion in the Twentieth Century*, p. 202; Johnnie Coleman, *There is no Hiding Place*" (Chicago: Universal Foundation for Better Living, Inc., 1990), pp. 2-7; and David Smallwood, "The Unique and Controversial Ministry of Rev. Johnnie Coleman," *Dollars & Sense*, 11, no 6 (December/January, 1985-1986), pp. 12-14 and 16-17.

51. Again, James H. Cone is an exception in this regard. See Cone, *For My People*, pp. 122-139.

52. Norment, *"In the Male Domain of Pastoring,"* p. 99.

53. Luke 4:18-21; Isaiah 61:1-2; Luke 10:38-42; Luke 13:16; Matthew 28:1-10; Luke 24:9-11; John 4:25-30; 20:16-18. The bible teaches that Jesus Christ came to redeem women as well as men. Women are co-laborers and are as worthy as men to perform and proclaim the duties of preaching the gospel and serving in a leadership capacity (John 1:12-13; Romans 8:14-17; 2 Corinthians 5:17; Galatians 3:26-28).

54. Loren Cunningham, David Joel Hamilton, with Janice Rogers, *Why Not Women? A Fresh Look at Scripture on Women in Missions, Ministry and Leadership*, Seattle, Washington: YWAM Publishers, 2000. pp. 13-239. The Bible teaches the full equality of men and women in creation and in redemption, thus they are mandated to share as equals in the Gospel ministry (Genesis 1:26-28; 2:18, 23; 5:1-2; Galatians 3:13.). The Bible teaches that the formation of woman from man demonstrates the fundamental unity and equality of human beings. The Bible also teaches that man and woman were equally responsible for the fall (Genesis 3:6; Romans 5:12-21; 1 Corinthians 15:21-22). Finally, the biblical mandate for women in ministry is found in Judges 4:4-14; 5:7; 2 Chronicles 34:22-28; Proverbs 31: 30-31; Micah 6:4; Acts 1:14, 18:26, 21:9; Romans 16:1-7, 12-13,15; Philippians 4:2-3; Mark 15:40-41; 16:1-7; Luke 8:1-3; John 20:17-18.

Chapter Five

Blazing New Paths:
Challenges for the Black Church and
Its Leadership in the Future

Just as womanist theologians must create opportunities to teach and share with Black church men and women, the Black church must create opportunities for womanist and other Black theologians to share with their congregations.

Kelly Brown Douglas[1]

I am delighted to know and affirm that there are some in our nation who have been on the cutting edge of making things happen. As we move closer to the twenty-first century, this same momentum will be critical to the transformation of this nation from its present state of self-centered individualism to one that truly embraces the intererelatedness of all life.

Bernice A. King[2]

Black churches and their leadership now stand at the beginning of a new century. Although many of the problems and challenges these institutions face are unprecedented, their primary function, as in the past, is to show, in word and deed, how God is at work in the world. To meet this mandate, black churches must constantly redefine and reform themselves and their ministries. Otherwise, they will become pathetic anachronisms in a world that changes daily.

117

The mission of black churches and preachers today and in the future lies not only in developing practical ways of liberating their people, but also in preparing them to survive in a world that is becoming wiser, more diverse, and increasingly uncaring. This chapter asks and seeks to answer the question that Martin Luther King, Jr. raised more than three decades ago: "Where do we go from Here?" The answer we provide to this question will determine whether or not the voice of the church is heard at all.

To Serve the Present Age:
The Black Church in Mission Today

The black church has long been perceived as the principal vehicle in the struggle against the many evils that undermine the quality of life in the African American community. The extent to which this remains true is open to debate, but nothing is more certain than the multitude of problems that confront it socially, economically, politically, and otherwise. Some of those problems have already been highlighted in this work, but others scream for attention.

The black church is still suffering from a shortage of well trained and progressive-minded leaders. Most black pastors are still ill-prepared to offer the church and community a vision of liberation for today and tomorrow. Although more young black ministers are going to seminary today than in the past, they are stunted nevertheless by the notion that following routine is better and more secure than presenting new ideas and mission priorities that are fresh and innovative. Indeed, the bitter fruit of routineness is rapidly rendering black churches weak and ineffectual. Thus, the first step that these institutions must presently take, as a precondition for mission, rests in preparing young men and women to do ministry and to act in the sacrificial style of Jesus Christ.[3]

This is all the more necessary considering the extent to which African Americans are abandoning the spiritual, moral, and communal values of their religious heritage in favor of the materialism and individualism of white Western society. Moreover, there is an increasing loss of a sense of the sacred in many circles of Black America, which finds expression in a lack of respect for the church, its teachings, and its leadership. Black churches must once again assume the role of teaching agents, using their time, energies, and resources to instill a greater sense of values in children, youth, and adults.

There is no greater mission in view of the gang activity, violence, drug addiction, and rising spirals of criminal activity that are destroying black youth from one part of the nation to the other. These problems are compounded by astoundingly high teenage pregnancy rates, single-parent households, the deterioration of the family and family values, and HIV and Aids epidemics that are wiping out young black females at frightening rates.[4] Even more unfortunate is the fact that black churches and their leadership are not coming up with viable solutions to this range of problems. Churches still view themselves as standing over against this world, and not as participants and agents in it. The common assumption among too many black preachers and pastors is that the world must transform itself to be fit for the church, not that the church must adjust itself to be a transformer of society and culture. The churches would do well to recapture the sense that God so loved the world that God sacrificed the best that God had for its salvation. This basic theological principle holds the key to a more viable mission in the world.

Black Churches are especially hard pressed to develop new models and understandings of ministry and mission that address the high rates of incarceration among black men and women. In the past, black churches and their leaders have left the responsibility for addressing this problem to social agencies. The fact that some church bodies are beginning to develop prison ministries constitutes a hopeful sign. The National Baptist Convention, U.S.A. has set up a program of outreach to black convicts, who comprise half the nation's prison population, that may well become the model for African American churches nationwide. Black preachers like Anthony Kelley, who heads the National Baptist program, are writing about this issue, with the intention of educating clergy and laity.[5] Gayraud S. Wilmore, one of the pioneer black theologians, have also written extensively on incarceration and rehabilitation as challenges to black churches.[6]

An equally pressing problem inheres in the problems of poverty and malnutrition that afflict poor black neighborhoods, in the inner cities and in rural America. Poverty and economic insecurity in these areas are greater than they were thirty years ago, when the last phase of the modern civil rights crusade attacked the economic roots of racism under Martin Luther King, Jr.'s leadership. These problems are enhanced by the lack of educational and job opportunities, and by apathy and a sense of meaninglessness. Although some black churches are educating their constituents in the practice of wise economics, few have extended this type of consciousness-raising beyond their own consecrated walls. The St. Paul Community Baptist Church of Brooklyn, New York, under the pastoral leadership of Johnny R. Youngblood, is one exception. The program instituted by this congregation, which targets black men and women with the message of economic self-sufficiency and well-being, offers an example that black churches must follow on a wider scale.[7] Furthermore, black churches might look more seriously at coalition building as an avenue to the further economic development of the African American community.

Dealing with the problems of poverty and economic insecurity would be counterproductive without some attention to the institutionalized structures that cause them. Unfortunately, these problems are not as easy to tackle as the issues of civil or constitutional rights were in the 1950s and 1960s. Those who control the purse strings of the economy are not prepared to engage in a redistribution of wealth and resources, so black churches must continue to preach self-help policies based on collective responsibility and action. This becomes all the more difficult in a black community that grows increasingly divided along class lines, but that sense of collective struggle that have always characterized the struggle for freedom, human dignity, and survival must be rejuvenated on some levels.[8]

Even as economic issues are taken into serious account, the churches in the African American community cannot afford to abandon their operations in the sphere of politics. The need to continue to educate African Americans about the political processes of the society and their responsibility with respect to them remains critical. Black churches and their preachers and pastors cannot afford the luxury of separating religion from politics, as is so often the case with white evangelicals and fundamentalists. This point cannot be overstated, since increasing numbers of African Americans are gravitating toward white televangelists and other proponents of conservative Christianity who either reject politics as the tool of the unGodly, or use politics to promote an agenda that has nothing to do with eradicating racism and classism.[9]

A retreat into enclaves of rigid, moralistic, fundamentalistic Christianity is too simple of an answer for the complex questions that surround the issues of black liberation and survival. The dangers of this posture are already evident in the preaching of Reggie White and other black ministers who are being used to perpetuate anti-gay and anti-female sentiment based on a narrow reading of scripture and tradition. Such persons, however well meaning in their efforts to advance the message and spirit of Jesus Christ, are not standing in the best tradition of the black church and its ministry. To the contrary, they are, perhaps unconsciously, feeding the type of bigotry and mental and spiritual enslavement that the most progressive black churches have always sought to eliminate. Strangely, black churches and their leadership have done little at this juncture to counter the surge of religious bigotry that is further dividing the American society.

The gospel of freedom that is the heritage of black churches and religious leaders is much needed in the society today. It is a gospel that affirms the freedom of every human soul to be what God created him or her to be. It is a gospel that embraces and uplifts, not one that condemns and castigates. It is a gospel that respects personhood more than things; that stresses the liberation of the whole person, irrespective of differences in race, ethnicity, and nationality. It is a gospel that is as old as Richard Allen and Jarena Lee, and as recent as Jesse Jackson and Willie Barrow.[10] The power and relevance of the black church depends in large measure on its willingness and ability to keep this gospel tradition alive.

With this tradition before it, black churches must do more to instill in their constituents a world perspective. This necessarily requires a sensitivity to and deep concern for the sufferings of persons across the globe. This means that the 40,000 children who die daily in various parts of the world of hunger, malnutrition, and disease should not be casually dismissed. It suggests that black Christians cannot succumb to the politics of silence as nuclear weapons are stockpiled in India, Pakistan, and even the United States. This is what Martin Luther King, Jr. had in mind when he said that the African American "must have a growing awareness of his world citizenship."[11] This is the idea conveyed also by his daughter, the Reverend Bernice A. King, who, in a recent book, challenged all Americans to transcend self-centeredness in the interest of a spirit that "truly embraces the interrelatedness of all life."[12]

The Black Church and Ministry Tomorrow: Considerations for Black Theologians

Black theologians are among the most ardent and perceptive critics of the black church and its ministry today. Some write in poignant terms about the authoritarian styles of black male preachers and how they are smothering the creative potential and mission outreach of church and denominational structures.[13] Others are disturbed by the sexism and homophobia that pervade the thinking of black Christians.[14] Still others speak of the anti-intellectualism of black churches, and of the lack of capacity these institutions have shown to translate a theology that is relevant into effective, practical action for the benefit of the oppressed. But as part of the church in the African American community, black theologians must bear some of the responsibility for its shortcomings along these lines.

It is obvious at first glance that black theologians need to do more teaching in the congregations with which they affiliate. Indeed, they are the ones most equipped for this task, especially since most black churches-and their pastors have little more than a Sunday School knowledge of God, religion, and the Bible, and how these might be related in productive ways to a range of human problems. Black theologians too often assume that what they have to share in terms of ideas and insights must be tailored only to the academy. By sharing their ideas and convictions in a language that is comprehensible to people at all levels of church life, they can become a vital force in helping their people to move beyond perspectives that keep them enslaved intellectually, spiritually, and socially. Moreover, they would become instrumental in bridging the chasms that still exist between black theology as an intellectual discipline and the folk theology rooted in black congregations. This is the message echoing through some of the writings of James H. Harris, who is both a seminary professor and a pastor in a black Baptist Church in Virginia.[15]

The intense training of young black males and females for dedicated and sacrificial ministry is another level at which black theologians can make much-needed contributions. In seminary classrooms, too little time is devoted to translating ideas about God into practical forms of ministry that can prepare people to deal effectively with the many problems and challenges that confront them daily. Furthermore, too many black seminarians finish their course of study with the assumption that what they have gotten in the classroom is irrelevant for pastoral leadership and ministry in the black church. Thus, they move into pastoral situations with the intentions of saying what has always been said and doing what has always been done. The opportunity for innovative leadership evaporates under the shadow of routineness. Black theologians cannot afford to adopt the postures of white theologians, for they live in a cultural milieu where the theoretical and practical must always come together.

It is equally significant to note that black theologians have not said and written enough about the responsibility of the black church and its ministry for African American children and youth. This helps explain why so many young persons in the African American community feel lost and insignificant. This accounts in part for the little value that they often attach to their own life and the lives of others. This is why youngsters turn to unprotected and frequent sexual relations, drug and alcohol addiction, suicide, and various criminal activities. In a society where three in every five black youngsters encounter the criminal justice system, there is no room for neglect and indifference on the part of the churches and their leadership. Black theologians could do much in terms of eliminating such problems by helping black congregations to educate children and youth about how they might best make their lives meaningful and productive.[16]

Another challenge for black theologians rests in assisting black churches to overcome their own internal oppressive structures. The oppression of African Americans over time has contributed to oppression within the group, and this is particularly evident in the positions that some black congregations take when confronted with the gay lifestyle and with women who assert their right to be ministers and pastors. Although theologians like James H. Cone, Delores S. Williams, Kelly Brown Douglas are treating these issues in their writings, they seem to show some reluctance to share their thoughts with black churches that have the greatest need to hear them. If they are right in saying that black theology emerges out of the black church, then it is to that context that they must theologize about the inconsistency between God and all forms of oppression.

James H. Cone has underscored the failure of black theologians to do the type of social and economic analysis required to assist black Christians in developing strategies to fight the evils of racism, capitalism, classism, and imperialism.[17] His reflections around this concern will remain relevant into the twenty-first century. Black liberation and survival depend in considerable measure on how perceptive black churches and their leadership are when it comes to understanding the sources of their oppression and the best means for eliminating them. Black theologians are the most equipped persons in the African American church to combine social and economic analysis, Biblical piety, and theological reflection in a style that prepares their brothers and sisters in congregations for the kind of prophetic action that assists in bringing the Kingdom of God to earth.

Cone's challenge to conservative black churches in 1984 is still needed today, because too many black pastors and their congregations tolerate racism and other injustices in society while riveting their hopes on the joys of heaven. Having a keen sense of what Cone calls "the liberating heritage" of the black church, theologians in the African American community must consistently challenge any understanding of the faith that forces black Christians into a posture of quietism and indifference regarding social evil. But they must do so with the understanding that fundamentalist and evangelical Christianity has some value in that it has long provided a release for the many pent-up frustrations and emotions of the oppressed.[18]

Black theology can be useful in preparing African Americans for interdenominational unity and cooperation, especially since it suggests that denominational identities are meaningless in our struggle for liberation and survival.[19] Caught up in power politics and their own institutional maintenance, most black churches have merely talked about the need for ecumenical directions and ventures while failing to create them. Although collective mission work promises much in terms of the social and economic advancement of black society, it means nothing if black churches are not willing to work toward common goals in a unified fashion. Denominational identity means nothing when people are hungry and persecuted because they are black.

Generally speaking, black theology must help provide a vision of the ideal society for the future of African Americans. That vision must indeed embrace the need for black unity, but it cannot stop there and be true to the demands of the Christian faith. It must also embrace the world. In other words, it must take into account the particularity of the black experience while taking seriously the universality of human experiences. This conviction courses through the theology of James Cone and J. Deotis Roberts, who highlight the need for African Americans to share and learn from the experiences of people worldwide while creating bridges of understanding, goodwill, and collective action against oppression.[20]

Black womanist theologians provide perhaps the best hope for a revitalization of the black church and its ministry and mission. As persons who know firsthand the triple evils of racism, sexism, and classism, they are well suited to provide a vision for the liberation of the whole people. Particularly important are the insights they can share, based on experience and training, with black churches and their leadership regarding the evils of sexism and gender oppression. They fully understand and are much more sensitive than black male theologians and ministers to the ways in which sexism blinds the visions of both men and women in the church and community as a whole. They know that some women, for example, are more vehemently opposed to female preachers and pastors than some men. In short, black womanist theologians must keep before the black church and its leadership a more wholistic and inclusive of black society and of the human family.

Some would prefer to see black theology as a fad baptized with Christianity. That perception has existed since the origins of black theology as an intellectual phenomenon in the late 1960s, but its maturation over time has convinced many to the contrary. However, black theology's survival in the years ahead will depend on the degree to which it speaks to the realities of human existence. In other words, it must remain an <u>existential theology</u>, and not merely something to be written in books and articulated in university and seminary classrooms. This invariably means that it must not abandon its obligation to speak to the needs of the oppressed and marginalized through the ministry and mission of the black church.

Endnotes

1. Kelly Brown Douglas, *The Black Christ* (Naruknoll, N.Y.: Orbis Books, 1994), p. 115.

2. Bernice A. King, *Hard Ouestions. Heart Answers: Sermons and Speeches* (New York: Broadway Books, 1997), p. 171.

3. One of the best and most perceptive discussions of the need to revive a pattern of young, educated leadership that has been broken since the time of Martin Luther King, Jr. is Clarence James, Leadership Development Patterns in the African-American Community, 1955-1979," in Carolyn Johnson and Ceola Baber, ed., *Black Social Philosophy in the l990s* (Lafayette, Ind.: Purdue University Press, 1985), pp. 55-61.

4. Michael Porter, *Kill Them Before They Grow: The Misdiagnosis of African American Boys in America's Classrooms* (Chicago: African American Images, 1997), pp. 1-76; Haki R. Madhubuti, *Black Men: Obsolete, Single. Dangerous?* (Chicago: Third World Press, 1990), pp. 1-271; and Na'im Akbar, *Visions for Black Men* (Nashville: Winston-Derek Publishers, Inc., 1992), pp. 1-87.

5. Anthony Kelley, *Jailhouse Religion: The Church's Mission and Ministry to the Incarcerated* (Nashville: The Sunday School Publishing Board of the National Baptist Convention, 1992), pp. 1-139.

6. Gayraud S. Wilmore, ed., *Black Men in Prison: The Response of the African American Church* (Atlanta: The ITC Press, 1990), pp. 1-158; Glorya Askew and Gayraud S. Wilmore, eds., *Reclamation of Black Prisoners: A Challenge to the African American Church* (Atlanta: The ITC Press, 1992), pp. 1-121; and Glorya Askew and Gayraud S. Wilmore, eds., *From Prison Cell to Church Pew: The Strategy of the African American Church* (Atlanta: The ITC Press, 1993), pp. 1-125.

7. Samuel G. Freedman, *Upon This Rock: The Miracles of a Black Church* (New York: HarperCollins Publishers, 1993), pp. 1-363.

8. This invariably means that the individualistic values stressed by black conservatives and neo-conservatives must be rejected. Such values are set forth in an unconvincing fashion in Shelby Steele, *The Content of Our Character: A New Vision of Race in America* (New York: St. Martin's Press, 1990), pp. 1-175.

9. African Americans seem to be becoming more receptive to the conservative Christianity promoted by televangelists. In 1981, one scholar claimed that most black Christian leaders did not support the agenda of the moral majority, but it seems today that some of the most popular black preachers have Television ministries that are carbon copies of those of white conservative televangelists. See William Willoughby, *Does America Need the Moral Majority: Where is It Leading Us?* (Plainfield, N.J.: Haven Books, 1981), pp. 128-132.

10. This gospel of freedom is treated brilliantly in the works of some black theologians, particularly womanists. For example, see James H. Cone, For My People: Black Theology and the Black Church -- Where Have We Been and Where are We Going? (Maryknoll, N.Y.: Orbis Books, 1984), pp. 122-207; Kelly Brown Douglas, The Black Christ (Maryknoll, N.Y.: Orbis Books, 1994), pp. 99-109; and Delores S. Williams, *Sisters in the Wilderness: The Challenge of Womanist God-Talk* (Maryknoll, N.Y.: Orbis Books, 1993), pp. 1-239.

11. Quoted in Lewis V. Baldwin, *Toward the Beloved Community: Martin Luther King. Jr. and South Africa* (Cleveland: The Pilgrim Press, 1995), p. 41.

12. King, *Hard Questions, Heart Answers*, p. 171.

13. The most trenchant critique along these lines is afforded in James H. Cone, *My Soul Looks Back* (Nashville: Abingdon Press, 1982), pp. 64-92.

14. Williams, *Sisters in the Wilderness*, pp. 206-234; and Douglas, *The Black Christ*, p. 100.

15. See James H. Harris, *Pastoral Theology: A Black-Church Perspective* (Minneapolis: Fortress Press, 1991), pp. 2-129.

16. One black theologian recommends "more dissemination of the teachings of nonviolence by Dr. Martin Luther King, Jr." among "children, teenagers, and young adults." J. Deotis Roberts, *The Prophethood of Black Believers: An African American Political Theology for Ministry* (Louisville: The Westminster John Knox Press, 1994), p. 71.

17. Cone, *For My People*, pp. 88-96.

18. *Ibid.*, pp. 83-85.

19. *Ibid.*, p. 85.

20. *Ibid.*, pp. 140-207; and J. Deotis Roberts, *Black Theology in Dialogue* (Philadelphia: The Westminster Press, 1987), pp. 7-120.

Dr. and Mrs. Nevalon Mitchell Jr.,
God daughter Shalena and Grandson Aaron.

About the Author

Dr. Nevalon Mitchell, Jr. was born in Wilson, North Carolina. He holds a Bachelor of Arts Degree in Sociology, a minor in Psychology and a Basic Intensive in Philosophy from the University of Michigan-Flint. He also has a Master of Divinity Degree from Garrett-Evangelical Theological Seminary in Evanston Illinois, where his special emphasis was on "The Church and The Black Experience", and a Doctor of Ministry Degree from The Presbyterian Theological Seminary in Louisville, Kentucky, where his Doctoral Thesis was "Black Preaching and The Black Church: Traditions Viewed in the Context of Liberation Theology".

He is licensed and ordained in The National Baptist Convention U.S.A., Inc. During his three years in seminary, he pastured the historic Woodlawn United Methodist Church in Chicago, Illinois. During his pastorate, the church experienced a rapid increase in membership, attendance and overall stewardship. He left Illinois in 1978 to enter the United States Army. In April of 1966, he joined the United States Army as a Private. He went through Basic Training at Fort Polk, Louisiana and Advanced Individual Training at Fort Gordon, Georgia. He served in Vietnam from March 1967 until January 1968. After graduating from college and seminary, he entered active duty as a Chaplain in March 1978. His military education included completion of the Chaplain's Basic and Advanced Courses, a year long Clinical Pastoral Education Course at Fort Benning, Georgia, The Combined Arms Services Staff School and The Command and General Staff College. He became a Fellow in the College of Chaplains and was listed in The People's section of Jet Magazine in June 1993. He is a graduate of the Surgeon General's

HIV Educator Course and was trained to be a member of the Trauma Crisis Response Team.

Dr. Mitchell's military assignments included HIV/AIDS Chaplain for the Eastern Region of the United States to include Puerto Rico and Panama, Senior Chaplain Clinician at the Walter Reed Army Medical Center, Washington, D.C., Deputy Brigade Chaplain for the Field Artillery Training Center, Fort Sill, Oklahoma and a two year tour in Korea during which his Chapel was designated the best of Eighth Army's 54 Chapels and won the Department of Army's Best Chapel from June 1989 to June1991, Staff Chaplain for the Residential Treatment Facility, Fort Gordon, Georgia, Chief and Deputy Chief for the Department of Ministry and Pastoral Care at the Dwight David Eisenhower Medical Center, Fort Gordon. Georgia, Assistant Brigade Chaplain, for the United States Army Armor Center and School, Fort Knox, Kentucky and the Assistant 4th Brigade Chaplain, Fort Carson, Colorado. His last military assignment was Staff Chaplain/Pastor Fort Detrick, Maryland. He retired from the United States Army as a Lieutenant Colonel.

He is currently serving as Staff Chaplain for the Department of Veterans Affairs Medical Healthcare System, Baltimore, Maryland. Dr. Mitchell was selected by the 2003 National Baptist Congress of Christian Education as an instructor in the Ministers' Division.

Dr. Mitchell appeared in the 1977 edition of The Outstanding Young Men in America. The Memphis Theological Seminary of Memphis, Tenn., requested and was granted permission to copy his Doctoral Dissertation for their library. His non-published article entitled "The Bright Side of Depression" was submitted to the United States Army Chaplains Review Board in 1986. Author of recent article, "Grief Resolution: Helping Others to Mourn" published in the December 2004 edition of The Christian Education Informer, National Baptist Convention, USA Inc.

Dr. Mitchell is a certified instructor in the Fourth and Fifth Steps, a world wide certified teacher in The Bethel Bible Series, a certified instructor for Adventures in Attitudes, Positive Image

Building, Positive Self Esteem and Positive Self Image, a world-wide certified Effectiveness Trainer for Youth, Parent, Leader, Teacher and Women, a Board Certified Chaplain in The Association of Professional Chaplains Incorporated, and a licensed certified Associate Counselor for alcohol and drug abuse.

His Professional Affiliations include The Association of Mental Health Clergy, The Association for Clinical Pastoral Education, The American Association of Pastoral Counselors, The American Counseling Association and The National Association of Alcoholism and Drug Abuse Counselors, The Department of Veterans Affairs National Black Chaplains Association and the National Association of Veterans Affairs Chaplains.

Dr. Nevalon Mitchell, Jr. is married to Wessylyne Kaye Mitchell and they are the proud parents of four adult children, seven adorable grandchildren and three God children. They are members of Meridian Hill Baptist Church in Washington, DC, Reverend Calvin E. Cage, Sr., Pastor.

He is the former Pastor of Faith Memorial Baptist Church of Charlotte, North Carolina.

Nevalon Mitchell, Jr. Ministries
Post Office Box 65
Bowie, Maryland 20720-4503
301-801-8361
E-mail Address: NevalonMJr@aol.com